THE FACEBOOK DIET

 GEMINI ADAMS

WWW·UNPLUGSERIES·COM

"A tongue-in-cheek look at our social media excess."
— *THE DENVER POST*

"Funny and true! An amusing look at our fixation with this phenomenon."
— *THE FEATHERED QUILL*

"A light-hearted giggle on how everyone's addicted to Facebook."
— *GEEK MAGAZINE*

"A humorous look at the common bad behaviors."
— *FAMILY HEALTH AND WELLNESS*

"Get on the Facebook Diet!"
— *CAMPUS CIRCLE*

Live Consciously Publishing

Inspiring, Mind-Altering, Life-Enhancing Media

www.liveconsciouslynow.com

THE FACEBOOK DIET

Published by Live Consciously Publishing, Ltd.
Registered Offices: 12 Clarence Terrace, London, NW1 4RD
www.liveconsciouslynow.com

ISBN: 978-0-9554656-3-5

Library of Congress Control Number: 2012910445

OH, HOW WE LOVE TO SHARE...

We, the human race, have taken evolutionary leaps in our ability to communicate, and in the way we share our stories, experiences, and wisdom. We've transitioned from cave drawings and smoke signals, to pigeon post, snail mail and telegraphs, to telephones, cell phones, email, video chat, instant messaging, and now social networks.

Mass communication has arrived. We can do it with anyone, anywhere, anytime! We've officially plugged ourselves in to the largest communications device ever known to mankind.

Rather than reaching out to connect with other planets or species (think moon and mars landings), and in the apparent absence of aliens—according to the White House—we've begun connecting with each other.

Cue soundtrack: Louis Armstrong... "What a Wonderful World."

Or is it? Facebook has been spreading across the continents faster than a highly contagious Asian bird flu, luring millions of members into the surreal world of social networking. It's big. Bigger than Justin Bieber or Ashton Kutcher's Twitter following. Hell, it's bigger than obesity and possibly just as lethal!

If you don't have a Facebook account yet then you are obviously, a) stuck in the MySpace or Friendster era, b) suffering from social media phobia, c) living in China, or worse, d) under a rock.

One person in every seven now has an account worldwide and Americans recently logged 101,000 years of Facebook time in a single month. On average, users worldwide spend thirty minutes a day updating, poking, chatting, posting, and tagging.

Still, the question remains: How good, bad, healthy, connecting, isolating, or addictive is Facebook?

Yes, Facebook has a dark side, one that can lead us into temptation, but it also provides us with an incredibly efficient and instant way to connect with each other for no cost! (Unlike cell phones.)

And—this is a big and—it has the potential to break down the social boundaries, uniting people across racial, religious, gender, and cultural divides in a way that has never before been possible.

You could say that Facebook is doing a far more effective job than religion at teaching us to "love thy neighbor," connecting us with random strangers and new "friends" from distant lands—people with different ideals, beliefs, jobs, traditions, even languages—all in the name of connectivity.

And, unlike when we first made contact with other races (armed with bows and arrows), Facebook is mostly the domain of friendly fire. The most damage you can really do is to "poke" someone (or post a really ugly picture of them!).

But, some people just can't get enough, can't have a conversation, can hardly manage a meal, or watch a movie, let alone a visit to the bathroom without "tagging," "posting," "poking," "liking," "commenting," or "chatting" on Facebook.

Yes, some people seem to exhibit rather unusual and alarming behaviors in relation to the world's biggest social network.

Hmmmmm......perhaps that was the plan all along? *To destroy the human race by ending real world social interaction and fuelling a narcissistic addiction to checking news feeds and notifications every few minutes!*

Just for fun we've been exploring the humorous side to our Facebook adoration (or is that addiction?) by observing and illustrating the many weird and wonderful high-tech habits that people exhibit thanks to Facebook.

Some might seem familiar.

Maybe they'll even remind you of someone. Do you hear yourself wondering, "I'll post this on Facebook and see what my 'friends' think?"

We thought so. Then maybe, just maybe, you're in need of a digital detox. Have a peek through these pages, you'll laugh at some, sneer at others, and occasionally wonder, "Am I a Facebook junkie, too?"

We suggest unplugging once in a while—it's a wonderful world out there, you know. Just lean down, grab the plug and pull. It's easy. Enjoy!

YOU KNOW YOU'RE A FACEBOOK ADDICT WHEN...

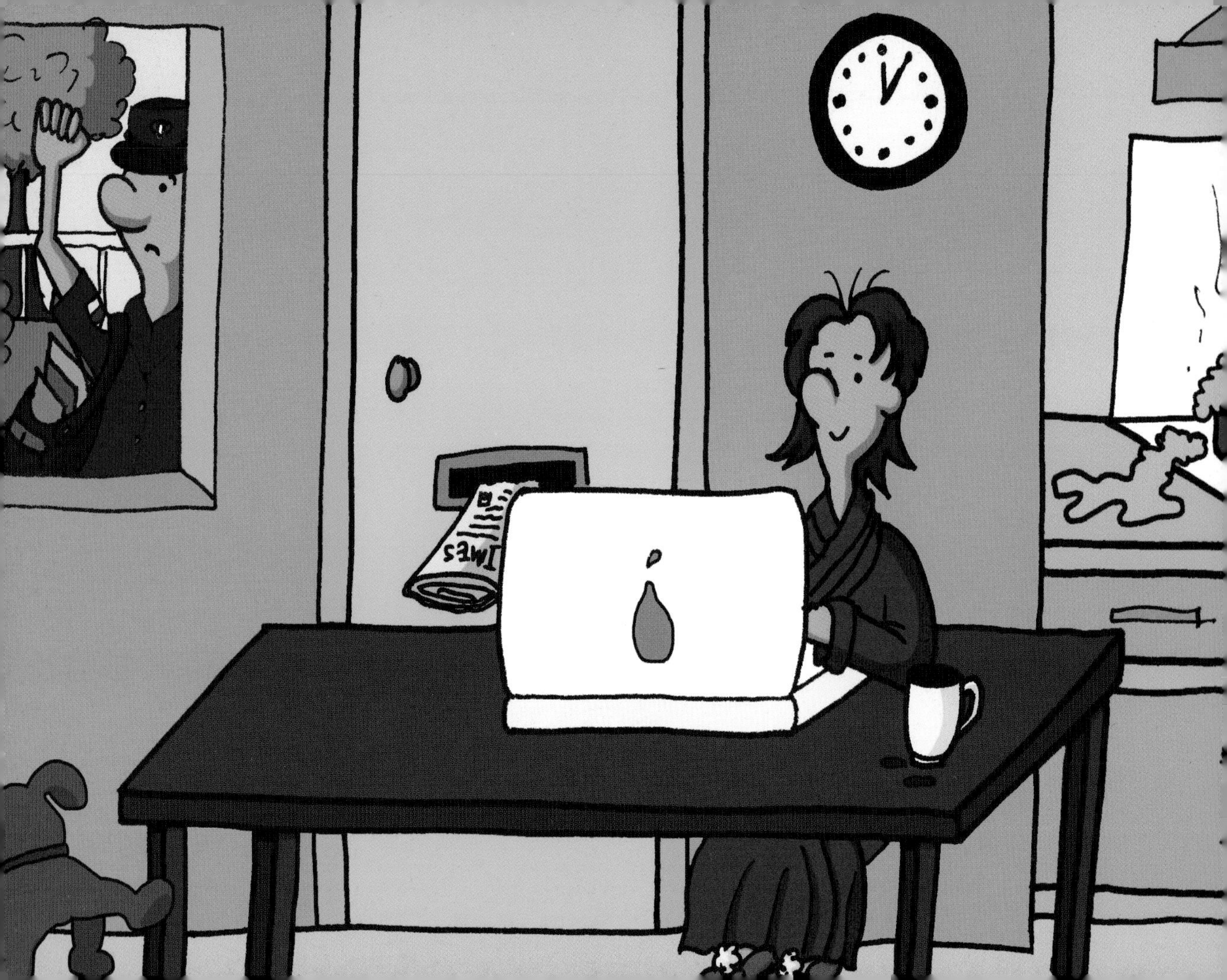

YOU OPEN YOUR ACCOUNT JUST TO CHECK FOR MESSAGES BUT FIND YOU'RE STILL SITTING THERE FIVE HOURS LATER.

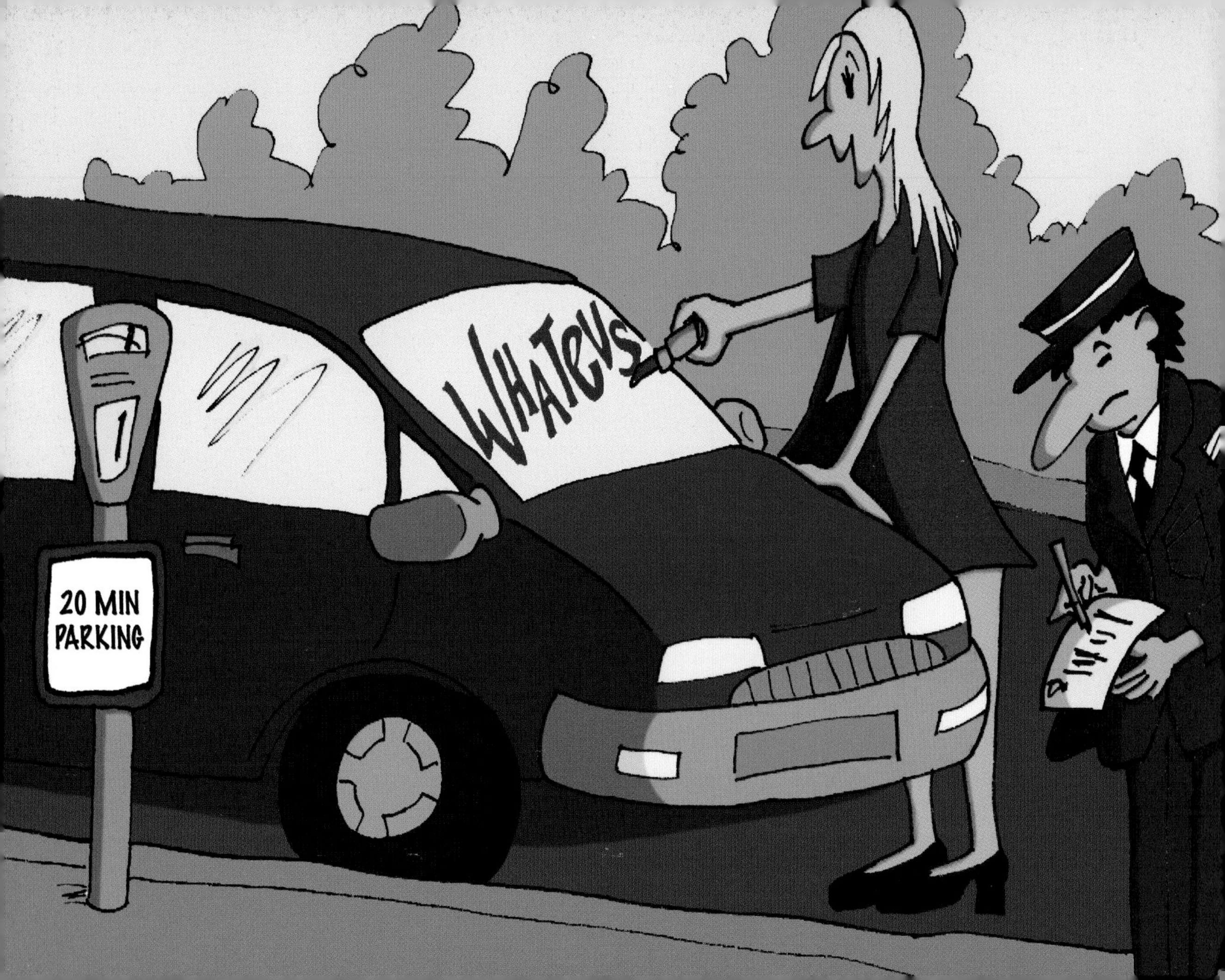
WHATEVS
20 MIN
PARKING

YOU'RE SO USED TO POSTING COMMENTS ON YOUR FRIENDS' WALLS THAT YOU'VE STARTED DOING IT EVERYWHERE.

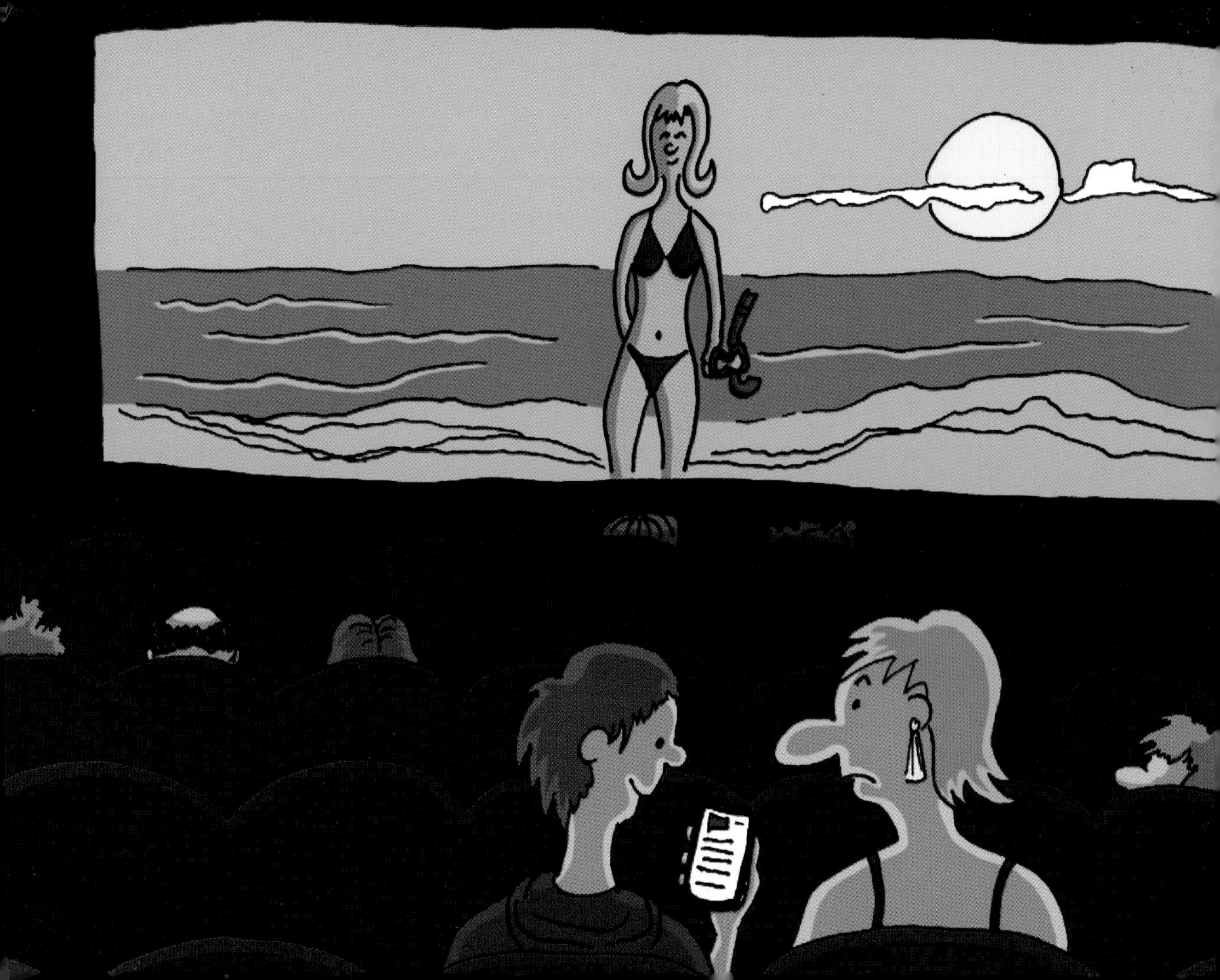

YOUR FRIENDS AND FAMILY GET ANNOYED WHEN YOU KEEP CHECKING FACEBOOK DURING THE MOVIES.

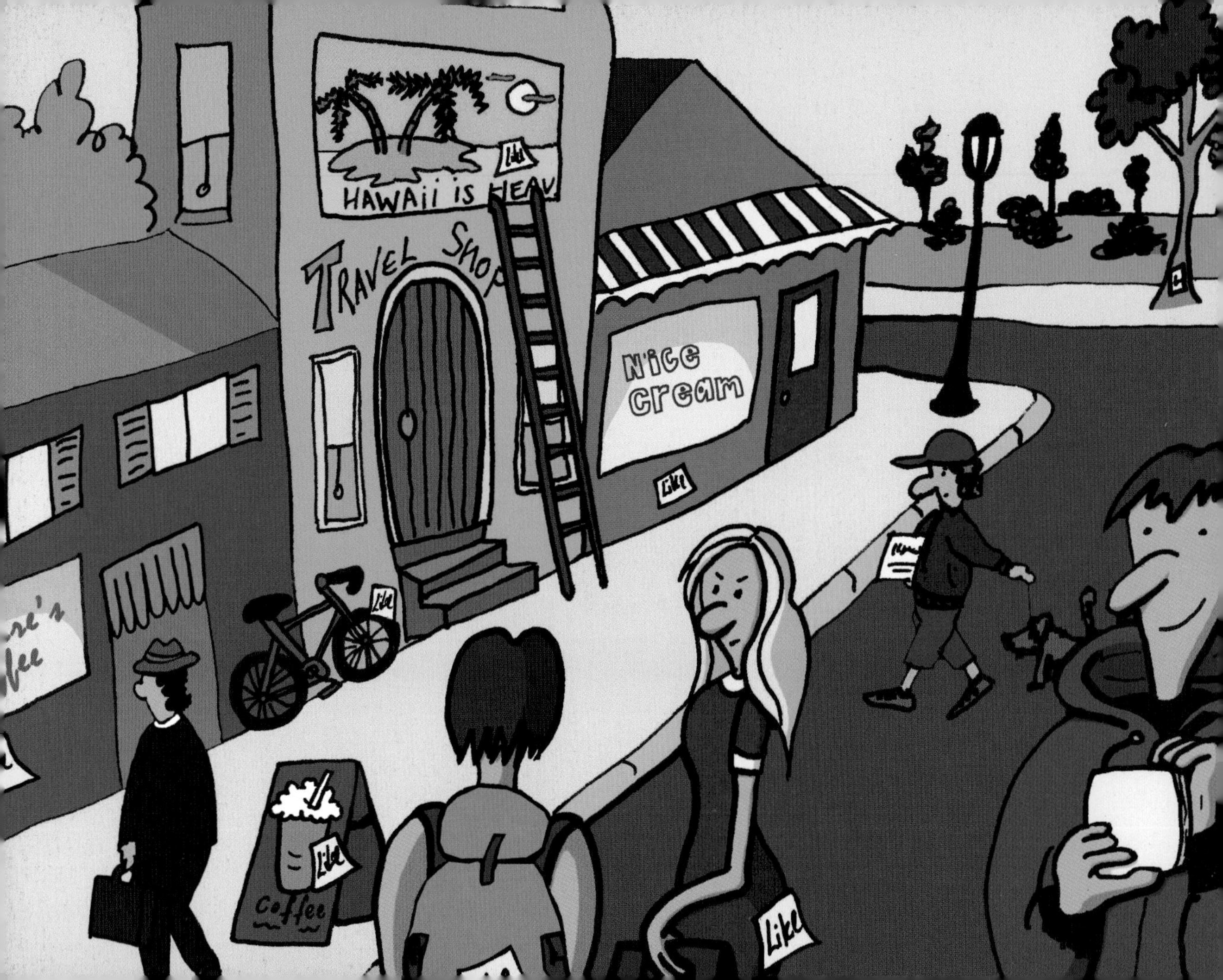
HAWAii IS HEAV
TRAVEL SHOP
Nice cream
Coffee

YOU'VE STARTED TO MARK THINGS YOU "LIKE" WITH POST-IT NOTES.

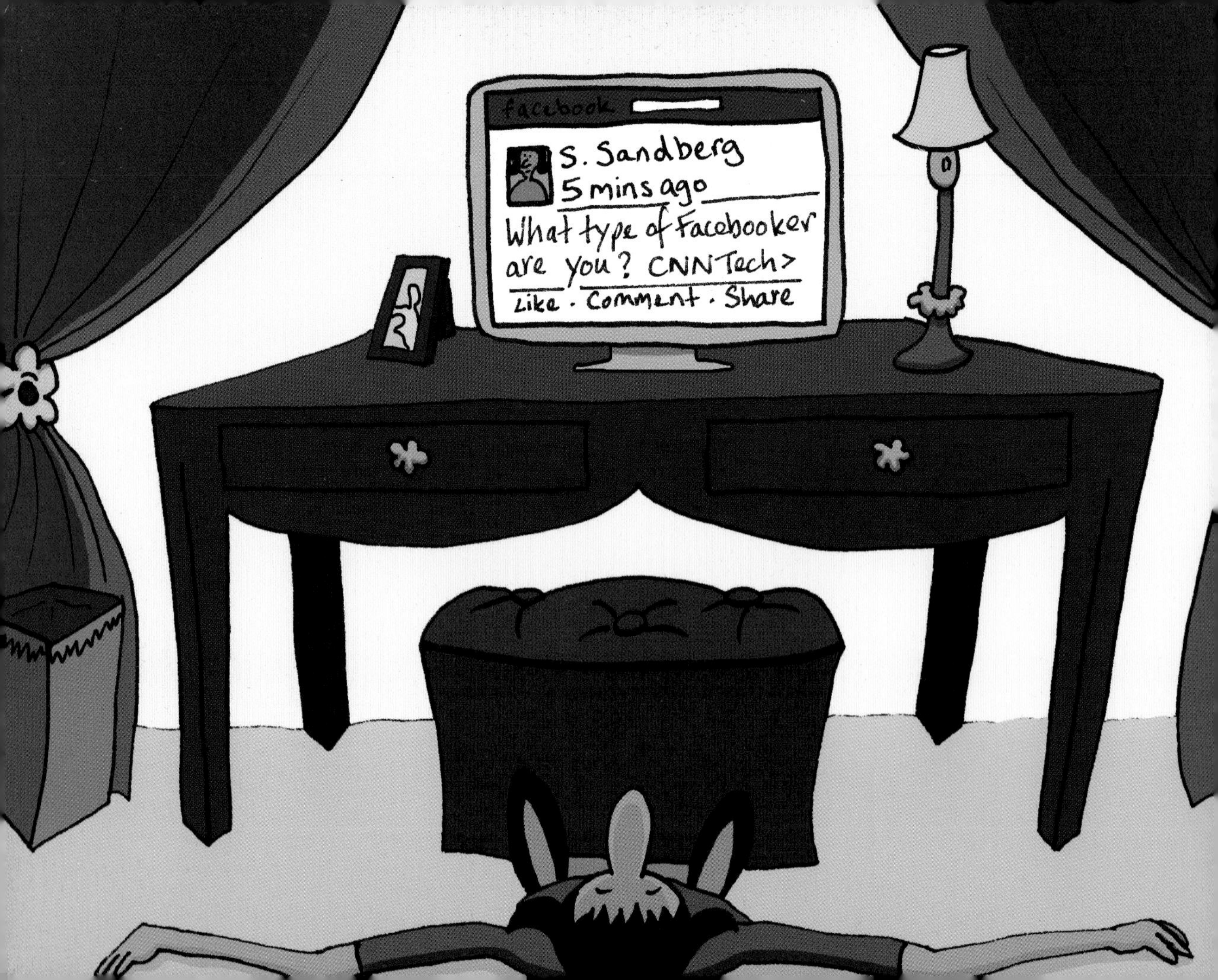
facebook
S. Sandberg
5 mins ago
What type of Facebooker are you? CNNTech>
Like · Comment · Share

YOU FAINT IF NONE OF YOUR 4,687 "FRIENDS" COMMENTS, SHARES, OR LIKES YOUR POST WITHIN FIVE MINUTES.

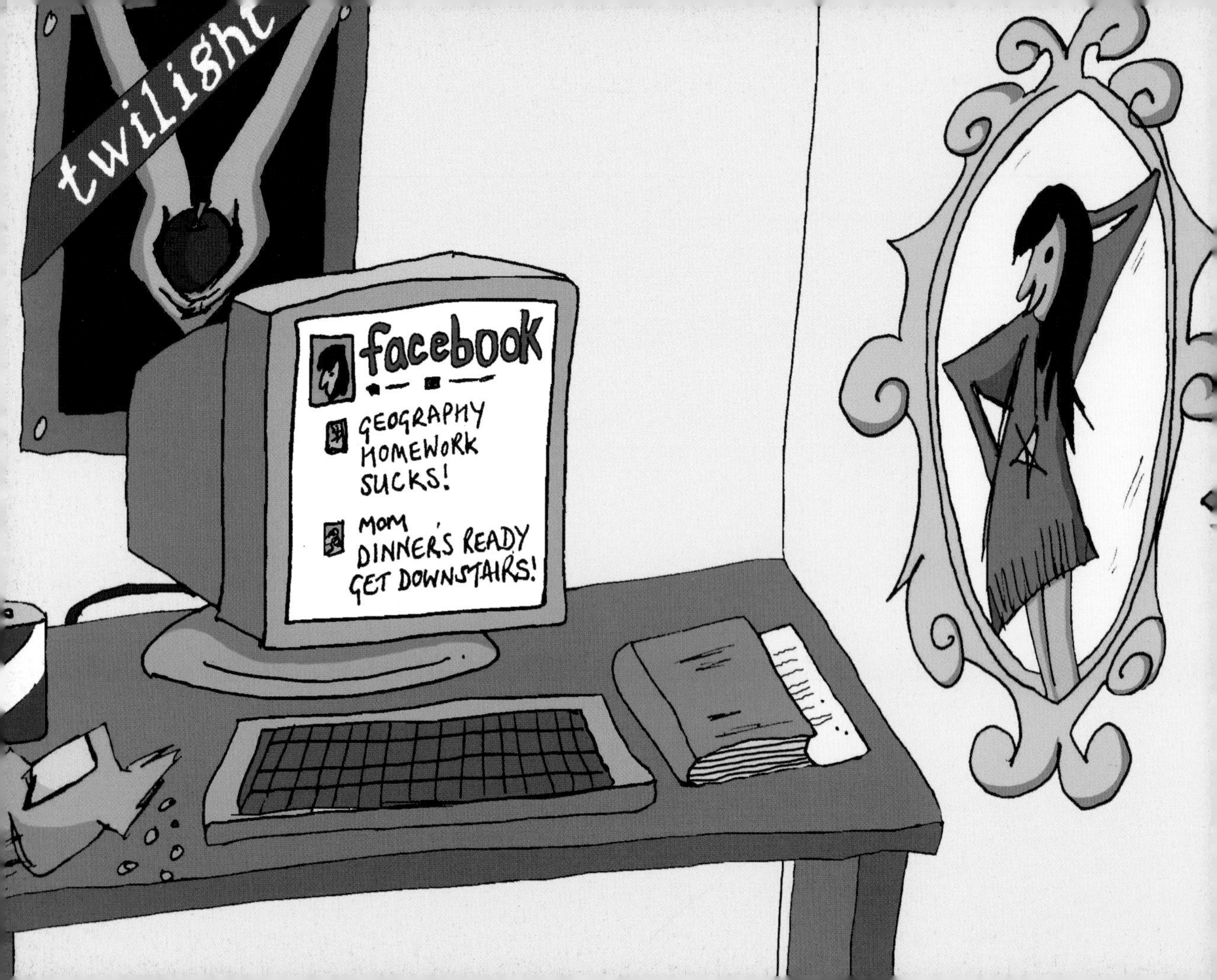
twilight
facebook
GEOGRAPHY HOMEWORK SUCKS!
MOM
DINNER'S READY GET DOWNSTAIRS!

YOUR MOM DOESN'T SHOUT "DINNER'S READY" IN THE DIRECTION OF YOUR BEDROOM ANYMORE, SHE POSTS IT AS A COMMENT ON YOUR WALL.

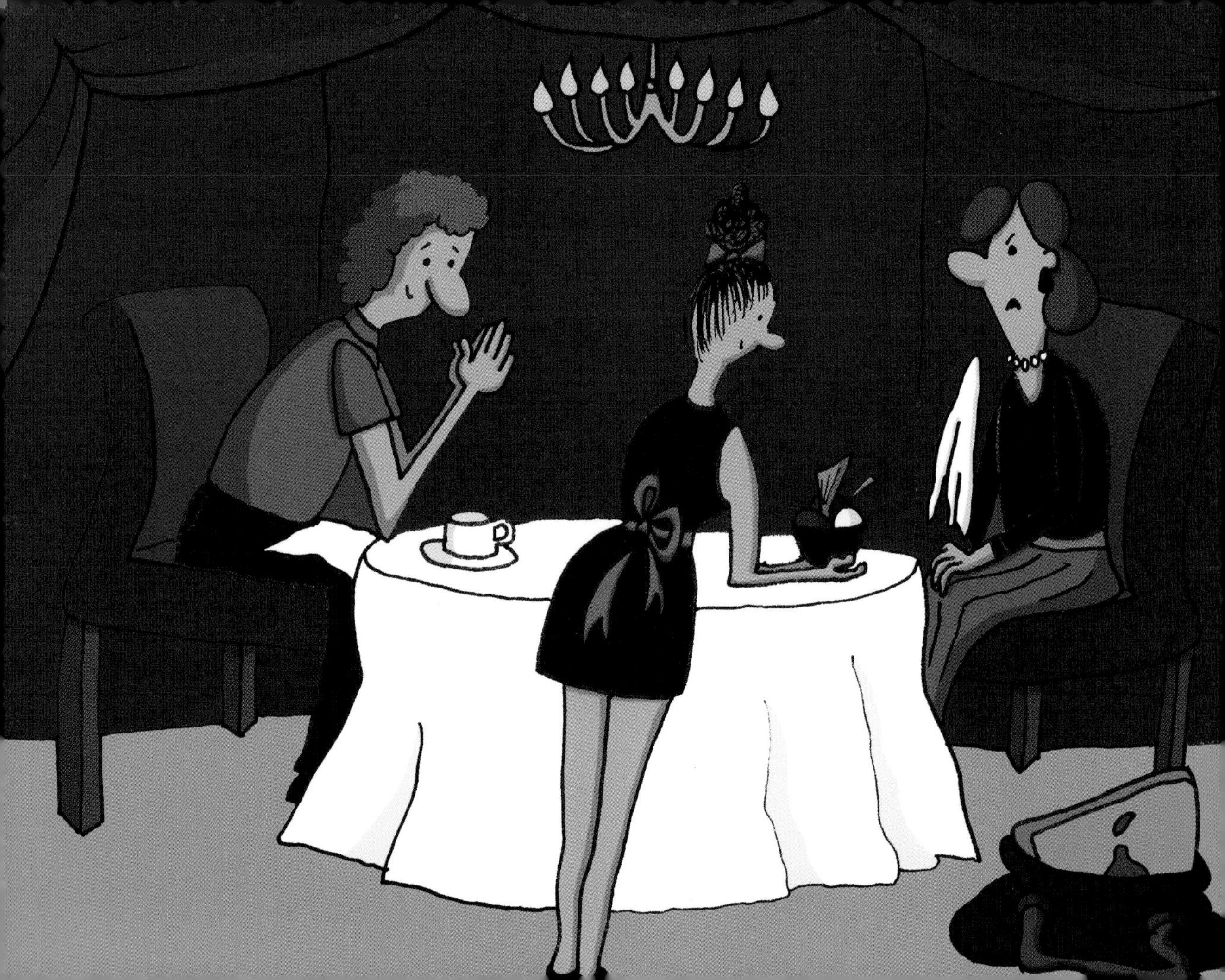

DURING THE FIRST DATE YOU POSE THE QUESTION: "SHALL WE UPDATE OUR PROFILES TO 'IN A RELATIONSHIP'?"

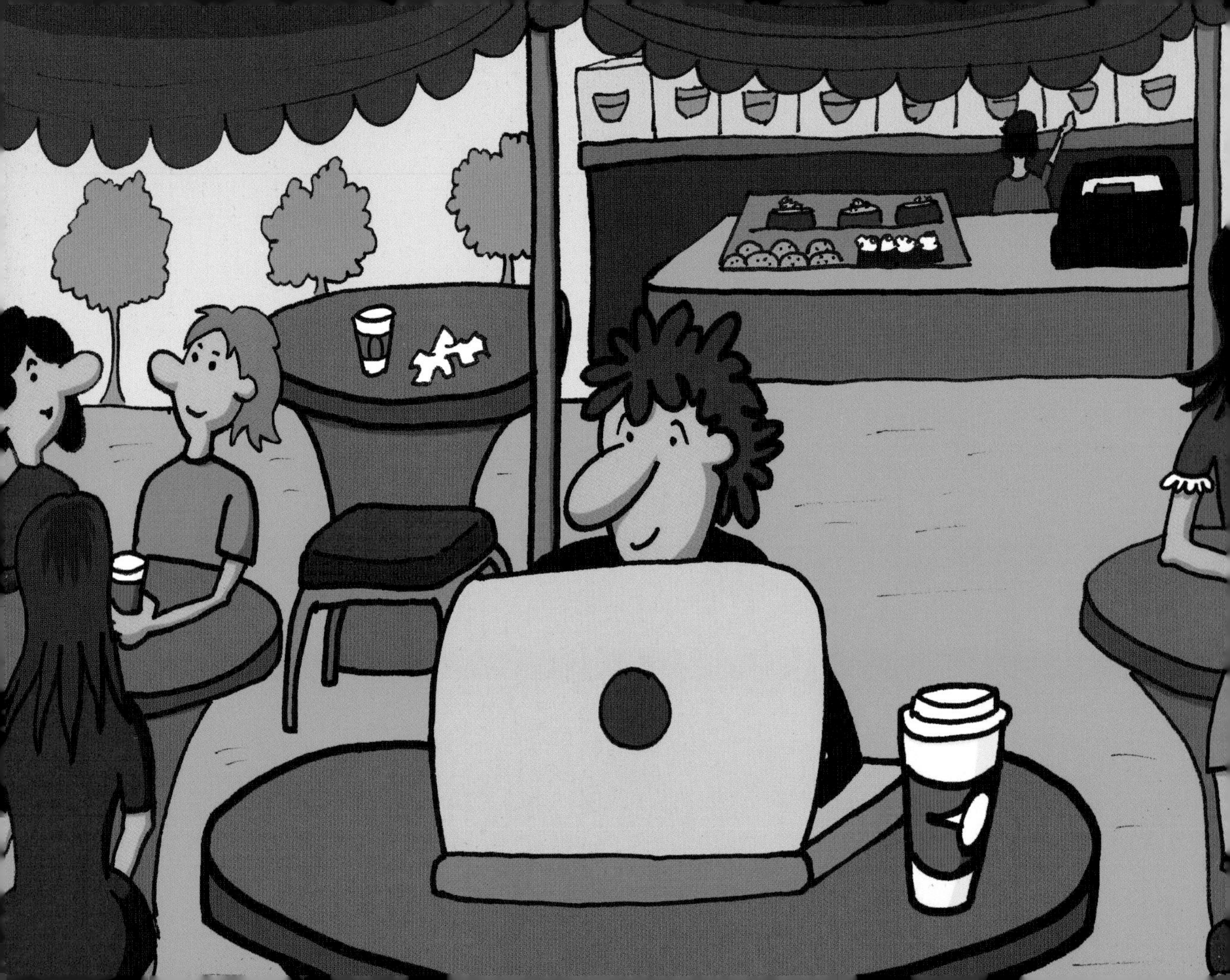

INSTEAD OF MEETING A FRIEND FOR COFFEE, YOU START A FACEBOOK CHAT ONLINE.

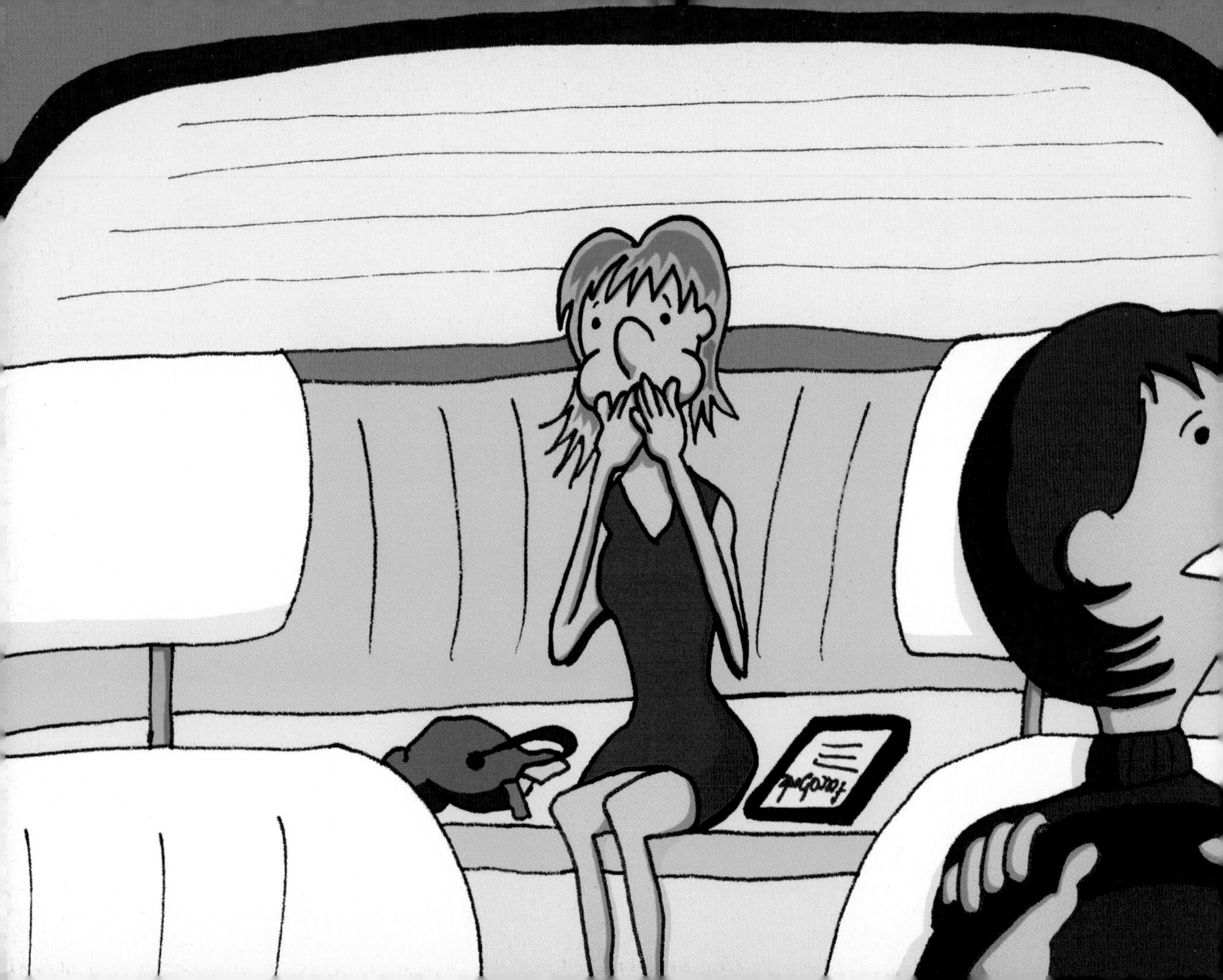

YOU GET CAR SICK ON EVERY JOURNEY BECAUSE YOU'RE BUSY CHECKING YOUR STATUS UPDATES AND NEWS FEED.

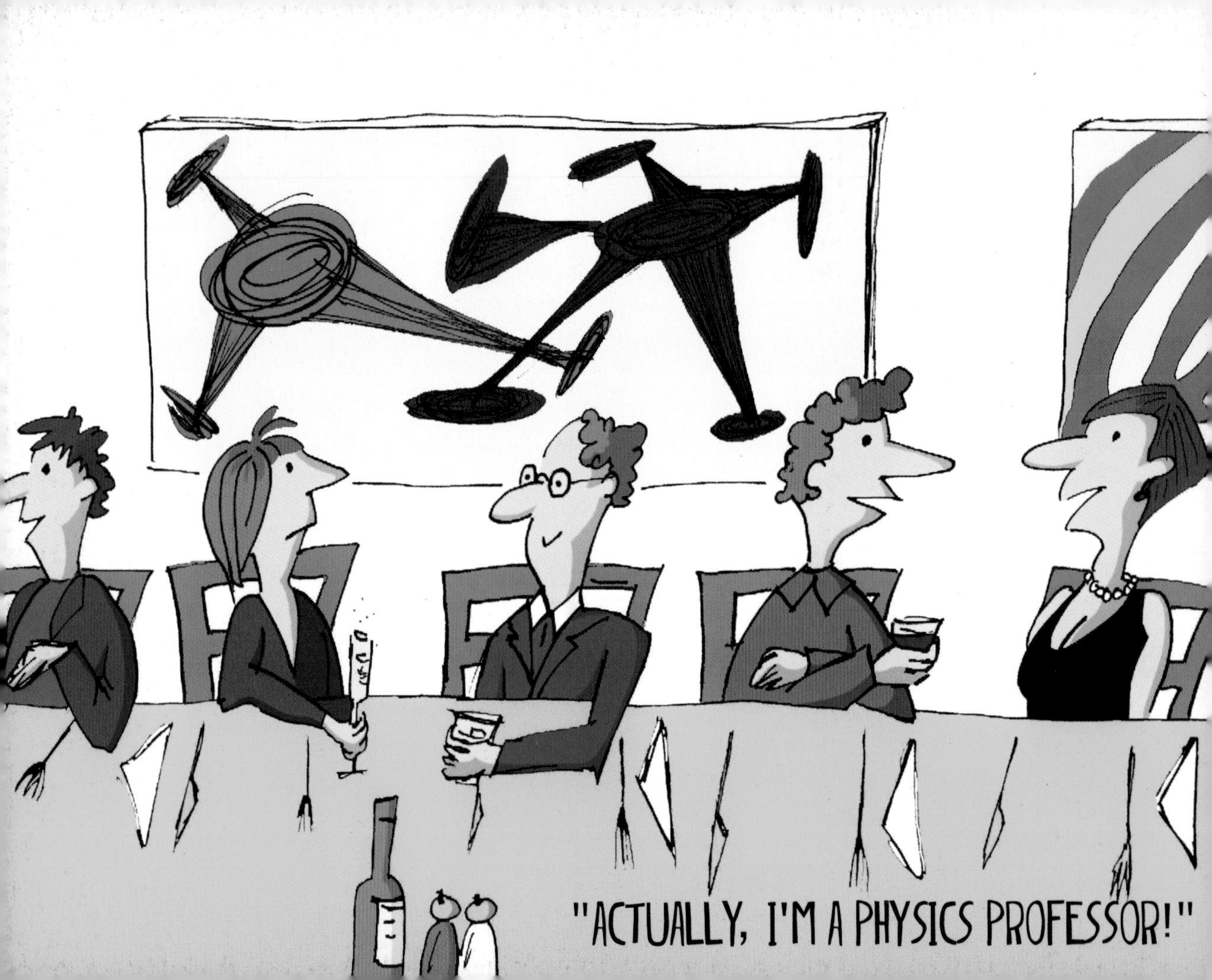
"ACTUALLY, I'M A PHYSICS PROFESSOR!"

YOU ASK PEOPLE ABOUT THEIR FACEBOOK STYLE . . . "SO, ARE YOU A 'POKER,' A 'LIKER,' A 'TAGGER,' A 'COMMENTER,' OR A 'PHOTO STALKER'?"

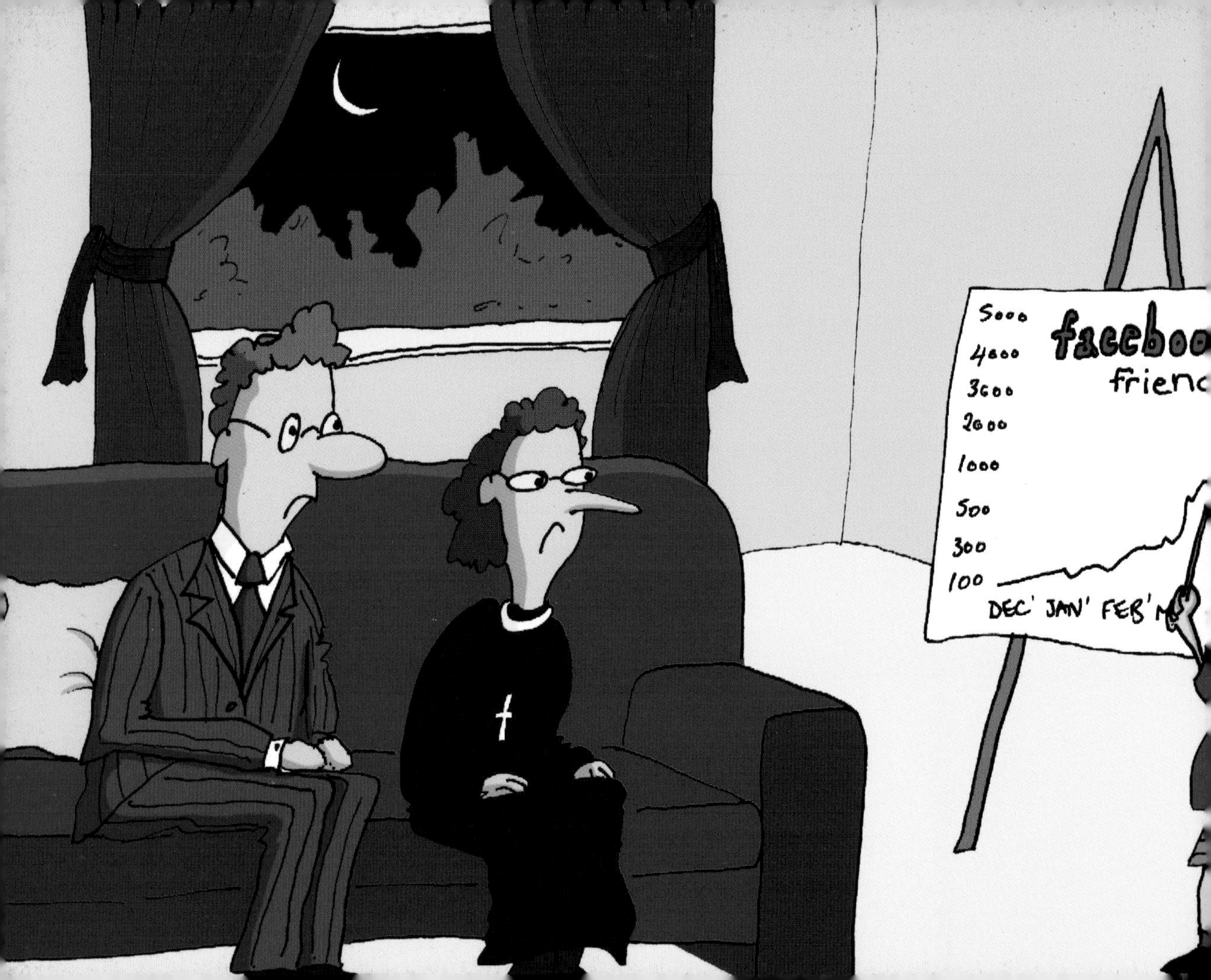
5000
4000
3000
2000
1000
500
300
100
DEC' JAN' FEB'

YOU'VE SPENT MONTHS REACHING THE MAGIC 5,500 FRIENDS — BUT NOW YOU NEED COUNSELING BECAUSE LIFE FEELS SO EMPTY.

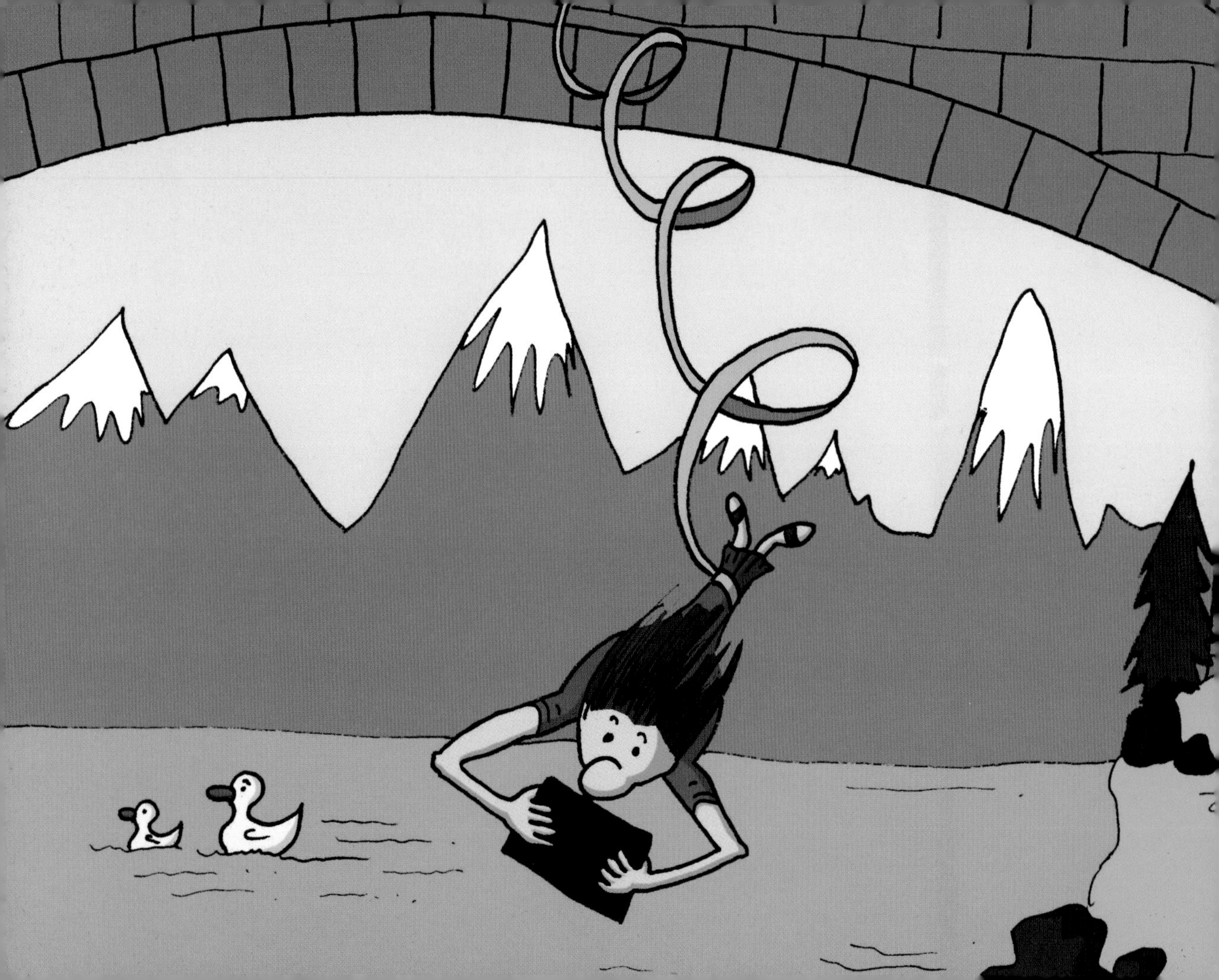

YOU CHECK IN WHEREVER YOU GO.

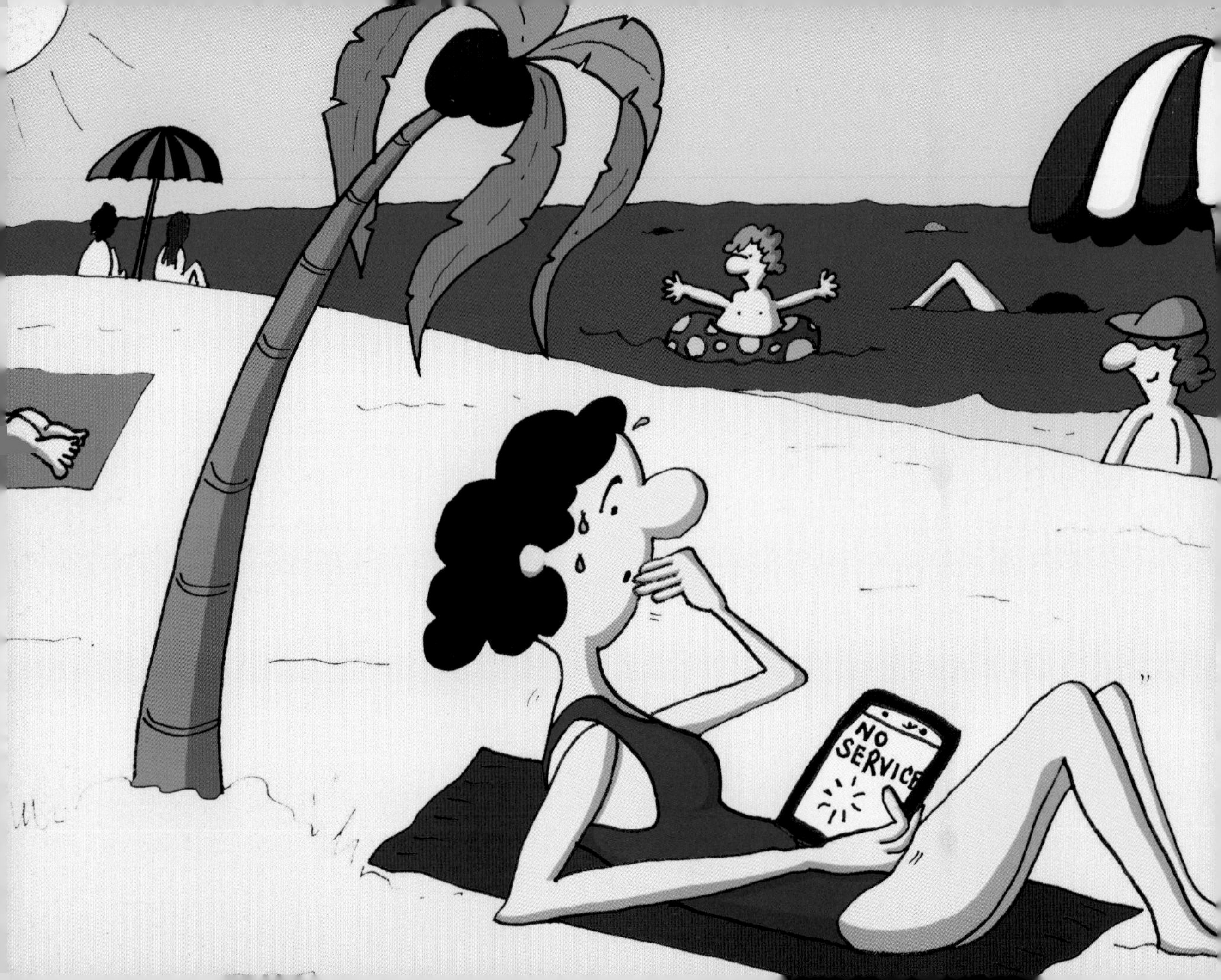
NO SERVICE

YOU SUFFER FROM WITHDRAWAL SYMPTOMS WHEN YOU CAN'T ACCESS YOUR ACCOUNT.

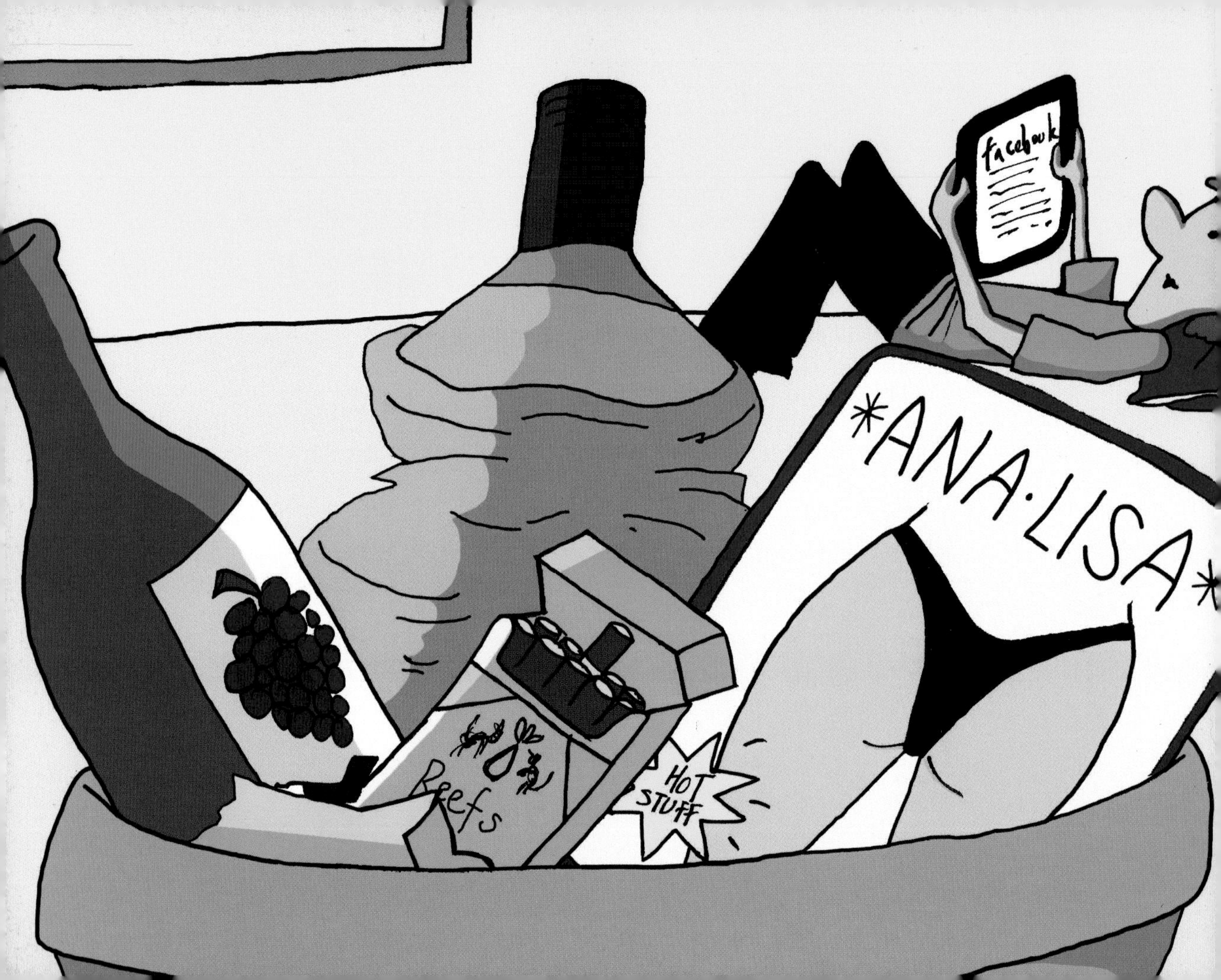
facebook
ANA·LISA
Reefs
HOT STUFF

YOU'VE GIVEN UP YOUR OTHER
ADDICTIONS - ALCOHOL, CIGARETTES,
WORLD OF WARCRAFT, AND PORN
- SO YOU CAN SPEND MORE TIME ON
FACEBOOK.

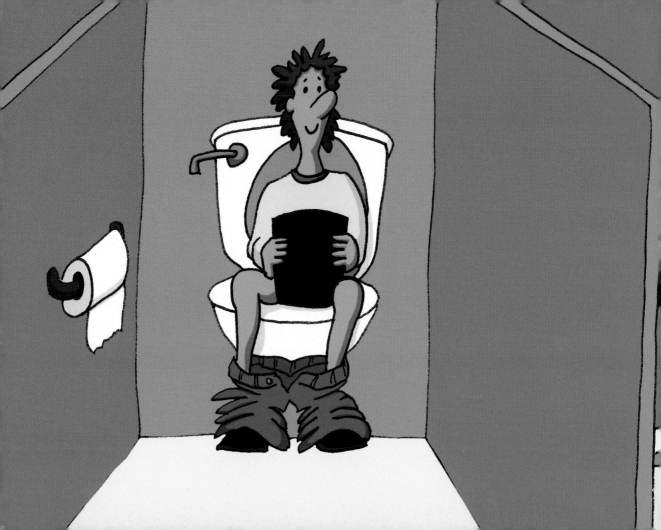

YOU'VE FAKED A BATHROOM VISIT SO YOU CAN CHECK YOUR MESSAGES.

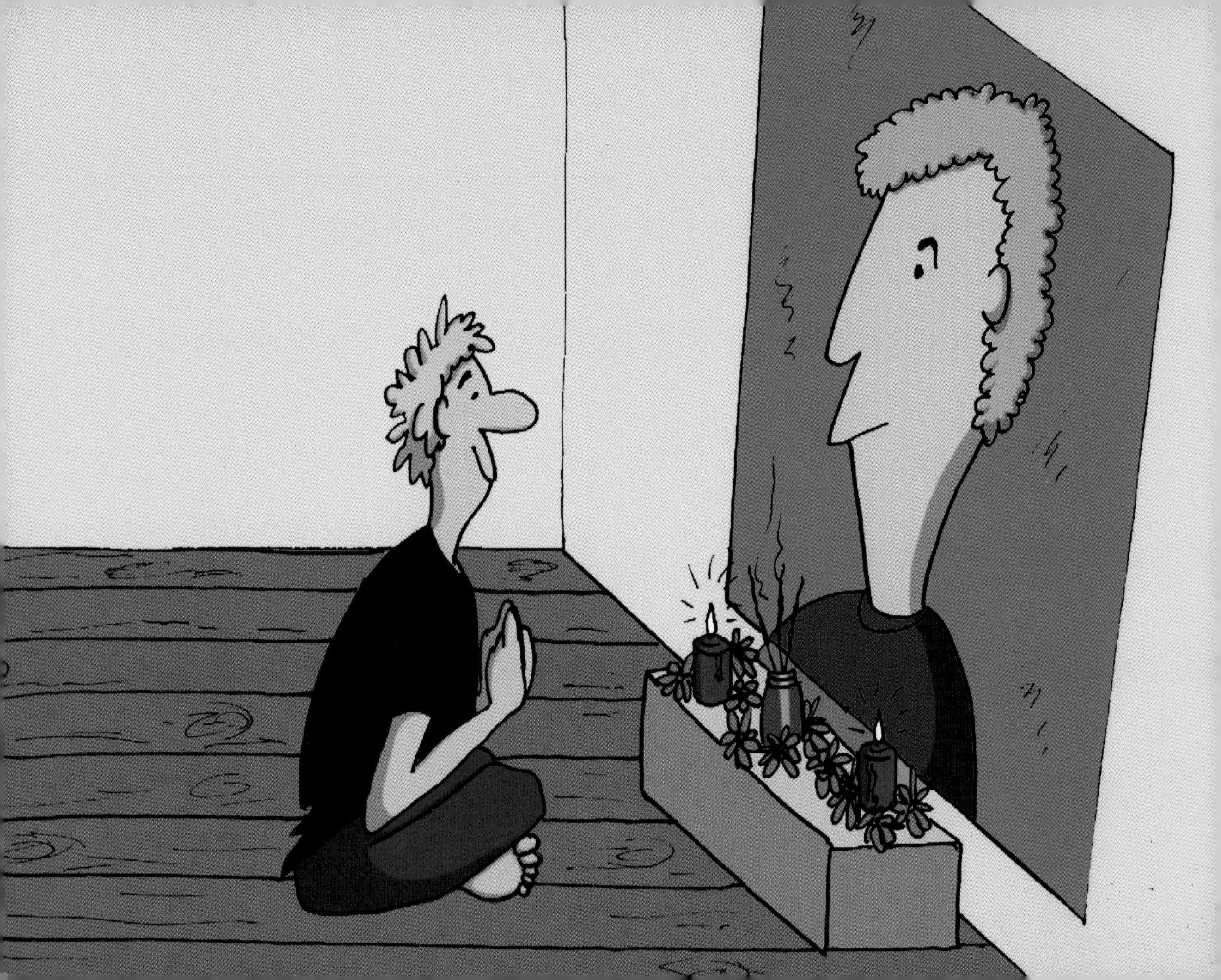

THE GURU YOU WORSHIP ISN'T THE BUDDHA, JESUS, OR ALLAH, IT'S . . . MARK ZUCKERBERG.

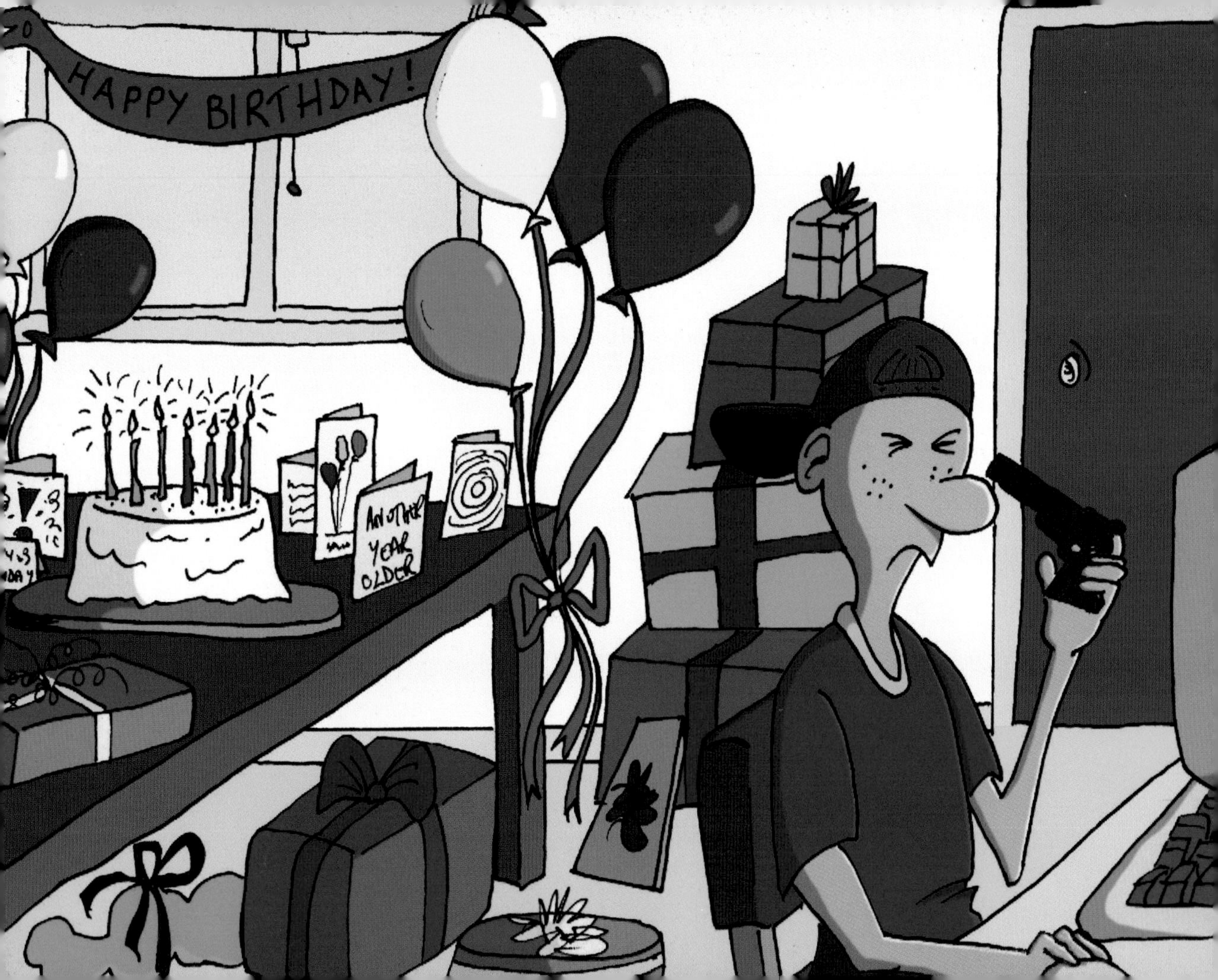
HAPPY BIRTHDAY!
ANOTHER YEAR OLDER

YOU'RE SUICIDAL IF YOU DON'T GET MORE THAN 200 HAPPY BIRTHDAY MESSAGES POSTED ON YOUR WALL.

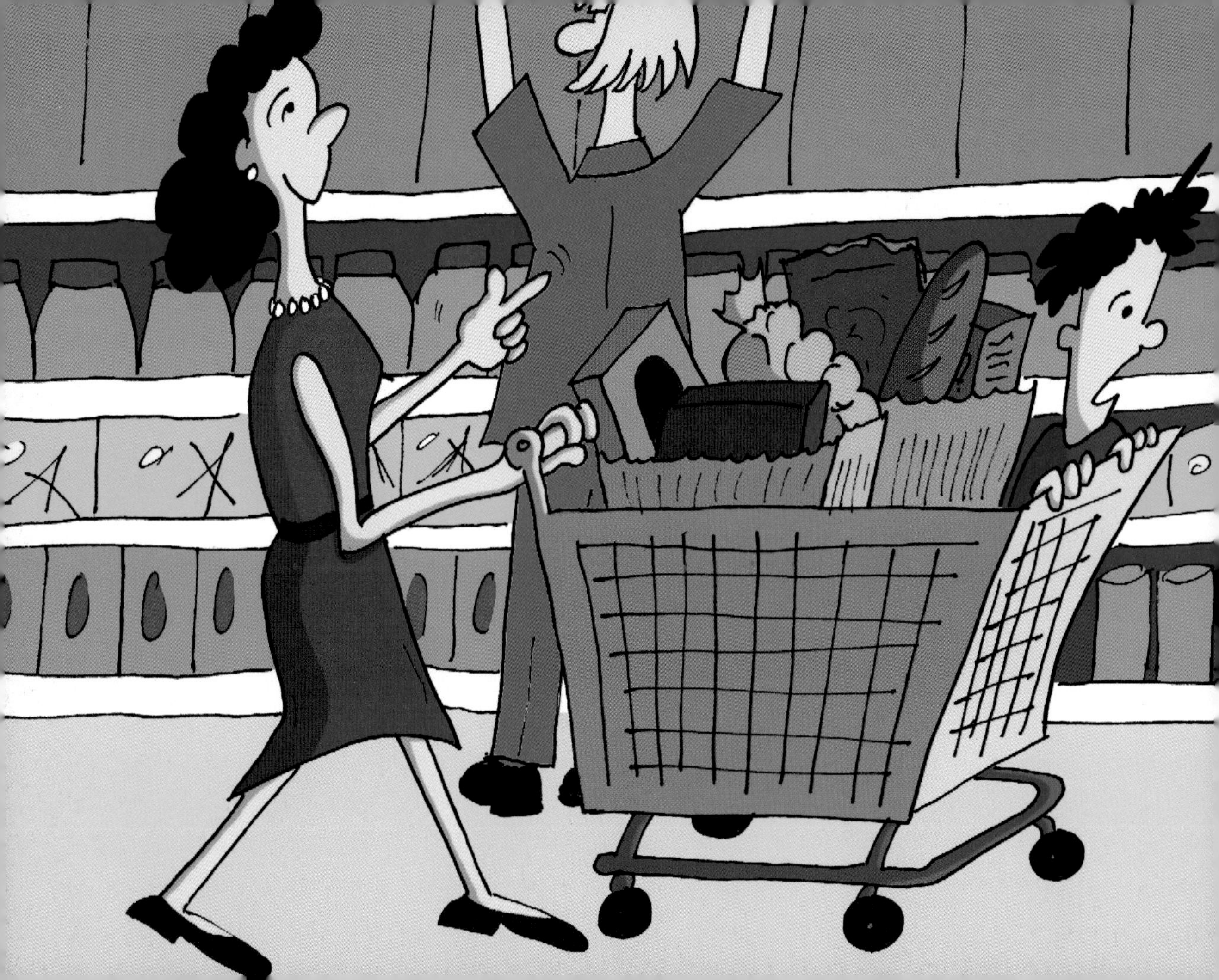

YOU "POKE" RANDOM STRANGERS WHEN YOU WANT TO GET THEIR ATTENTION.

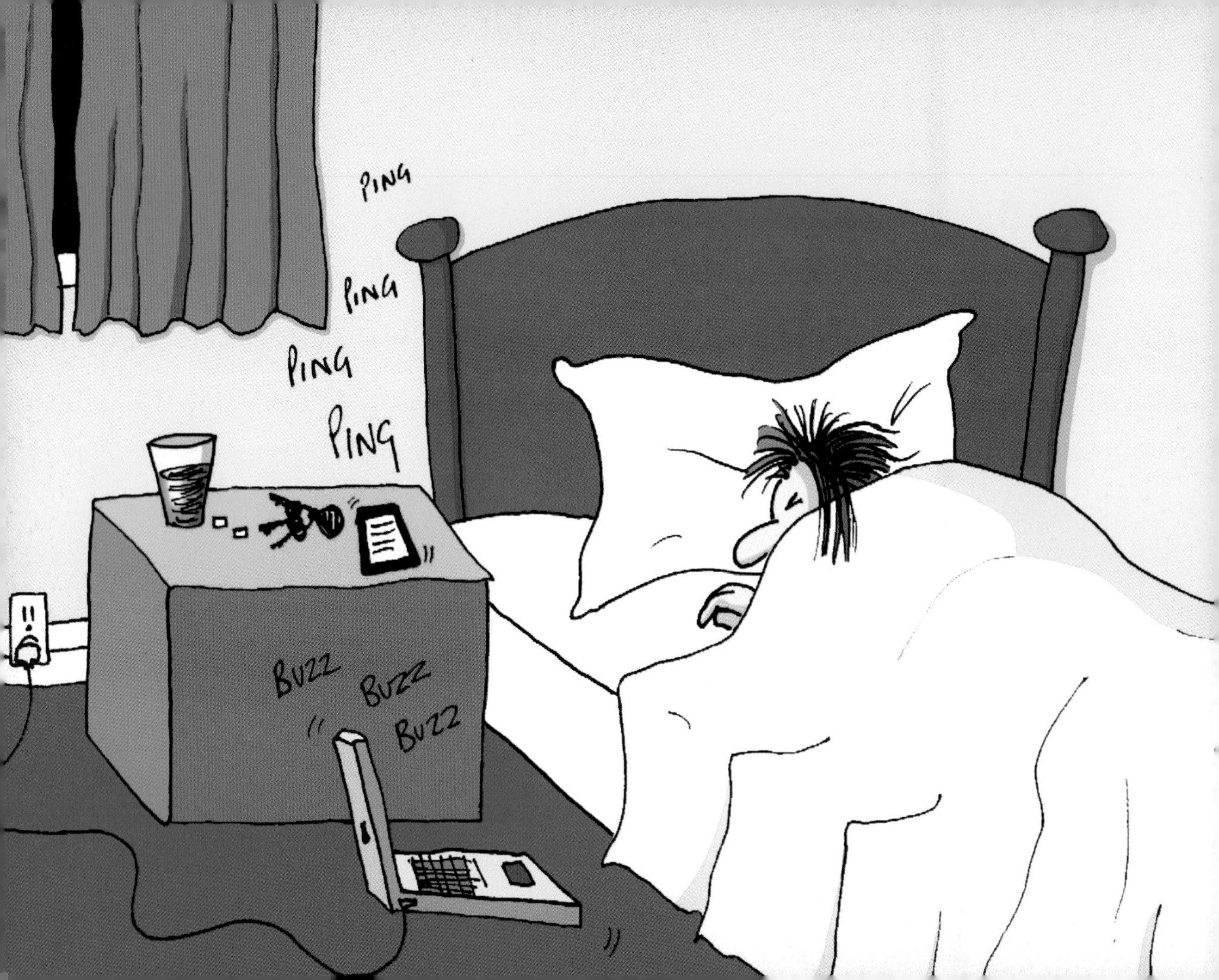
PING
PING
PING
PING
BUZZ
BUZZ
BUZZ

AFTER A "GREAT" NIGHT OUT, YOU AWAKE, NOT TO THE ALARM, BUT TO HUNDREDS OF NEW FRIEND REQUESTS AND TAGS IN SOME REALLY EMBARASSING PHOTOS.

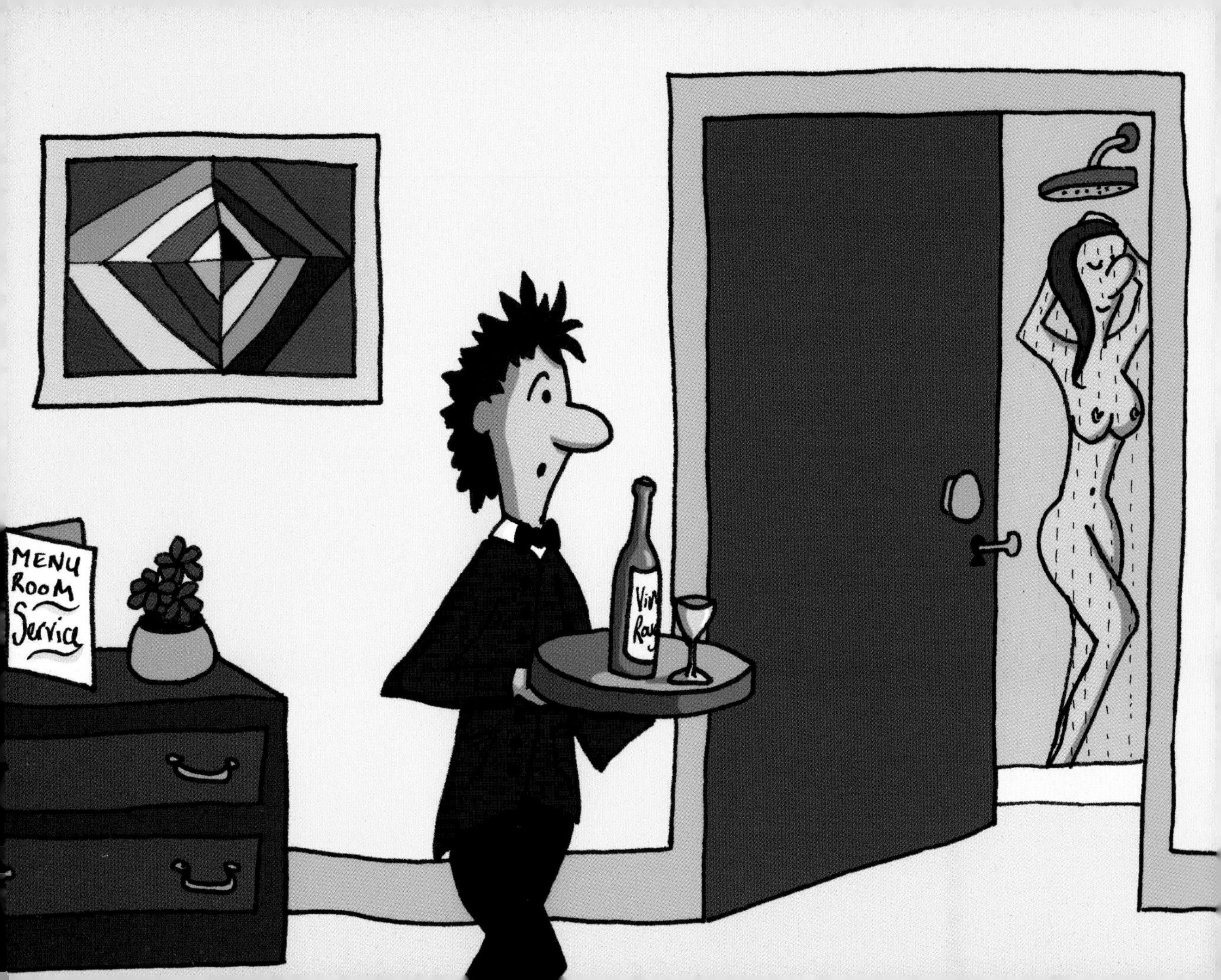
MENU
ROOM
Service

NOTHING SEEMS REAL UNTIL YOU'VE POSTED IT ON FACEBOOK.

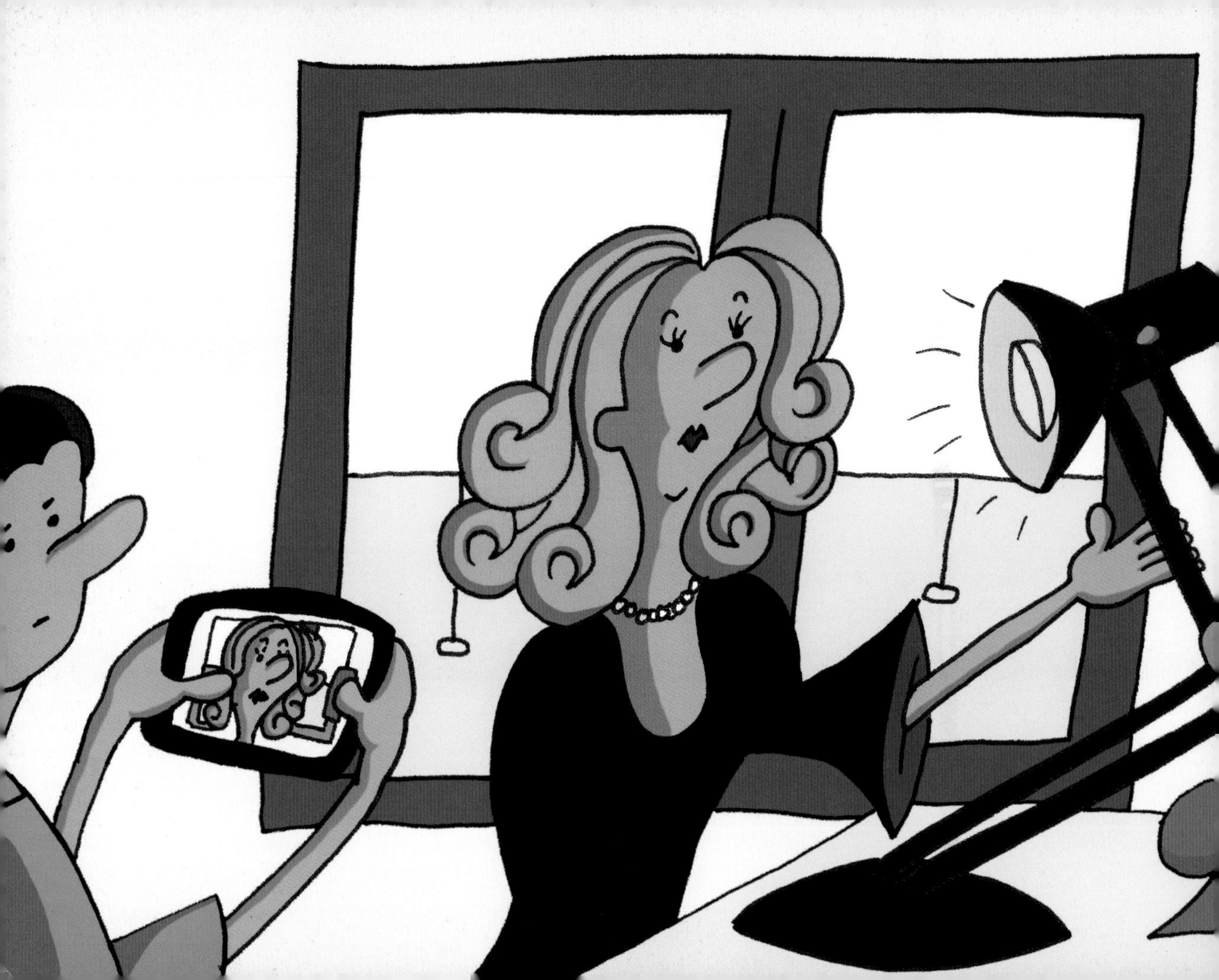

YOU ART-DIRECT WHEN SOMEONE'S TAKING YOUR PHOTO SO IT'S PERFECT FOR YOUR NEXT PROFILE PICTURE.

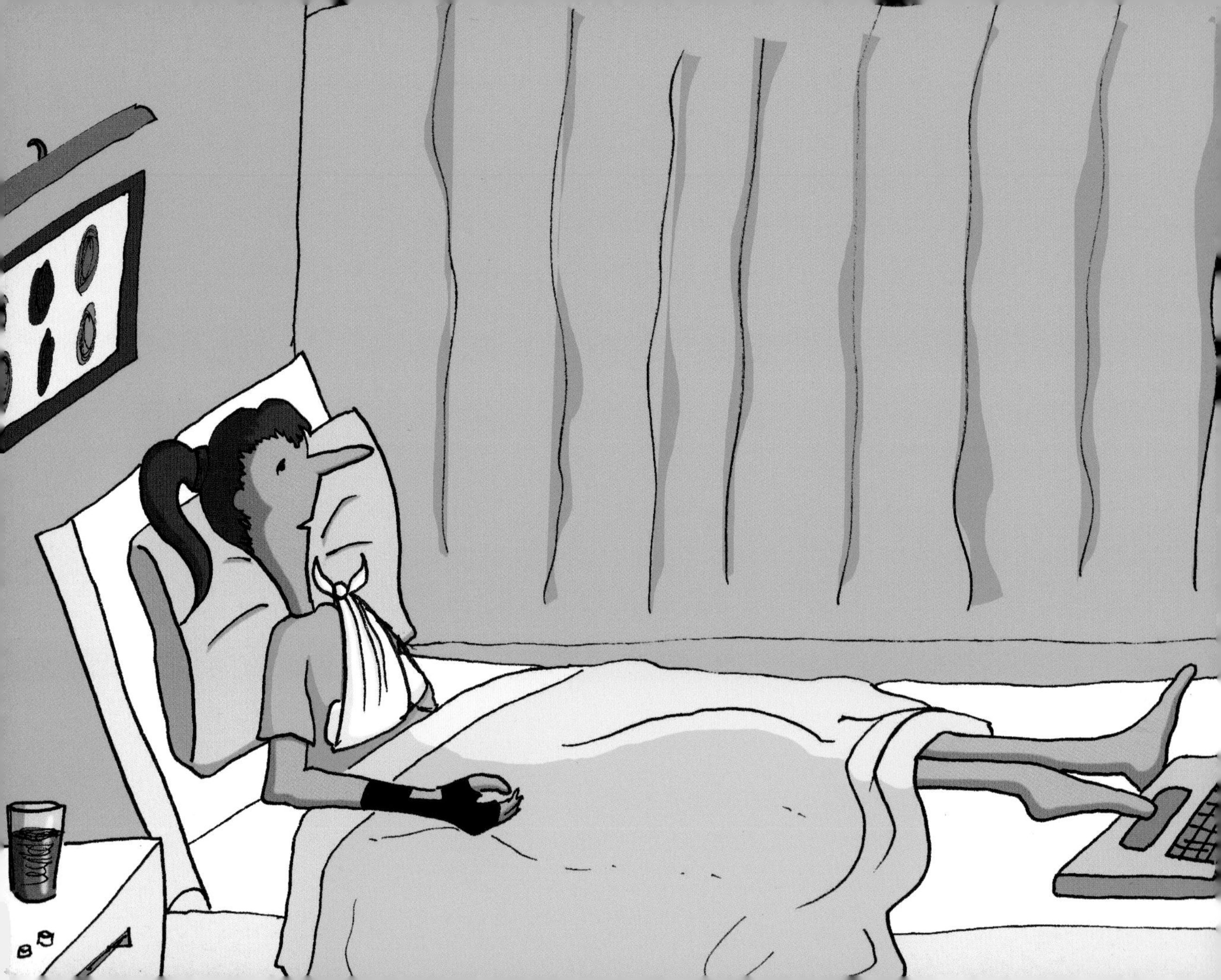

YOU SUFFER FROM REPETITIVE STRAIN INJURY FROM EXCESSIVE USE OF YOUR TABLET, LAPTOP, OR SMARTPHONE.

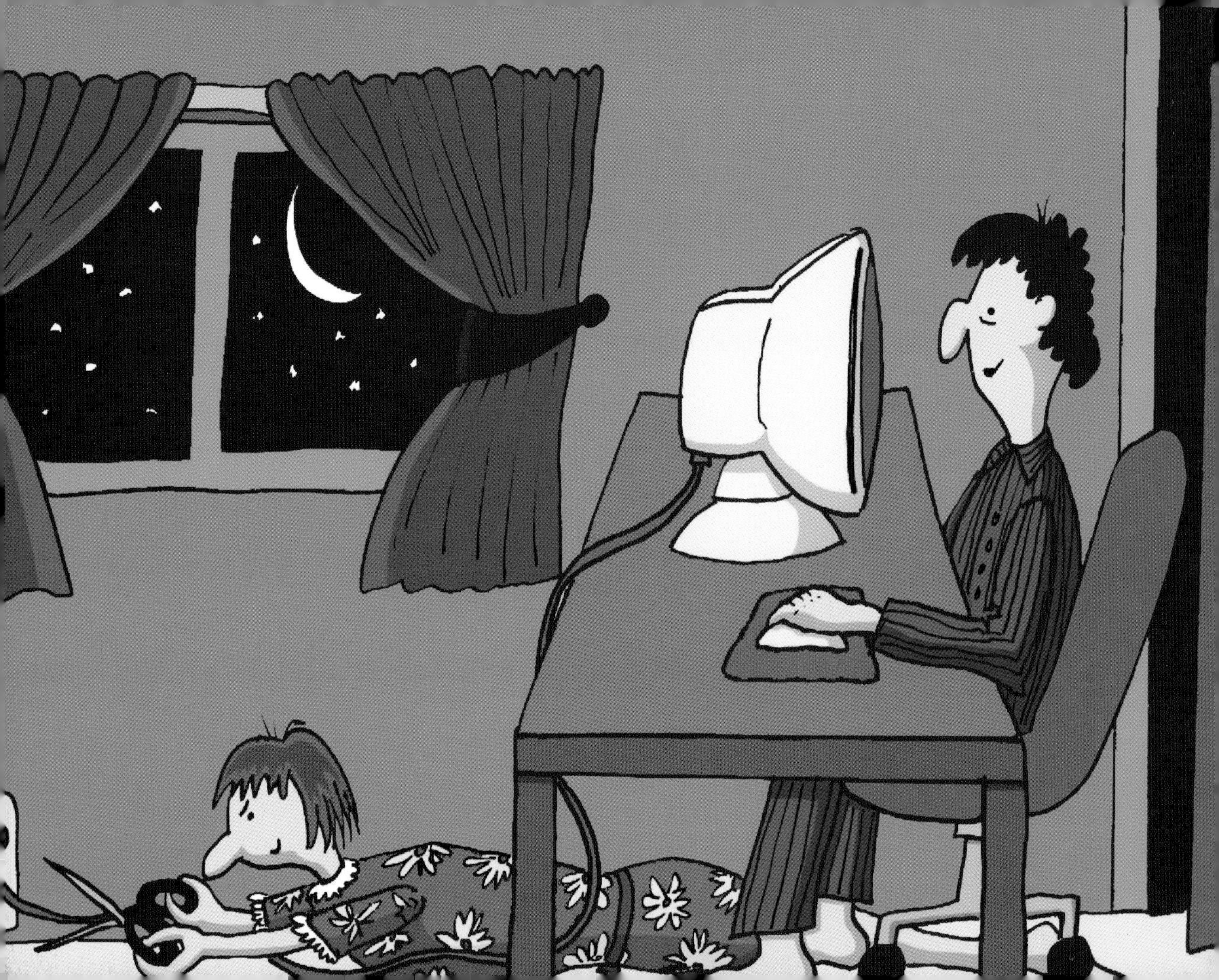

YOUR LOVED ONES GET REALLY CRAZY OVER THE AMOUNT OF TIME YOU SPEND GLUED TO A SCREEN.

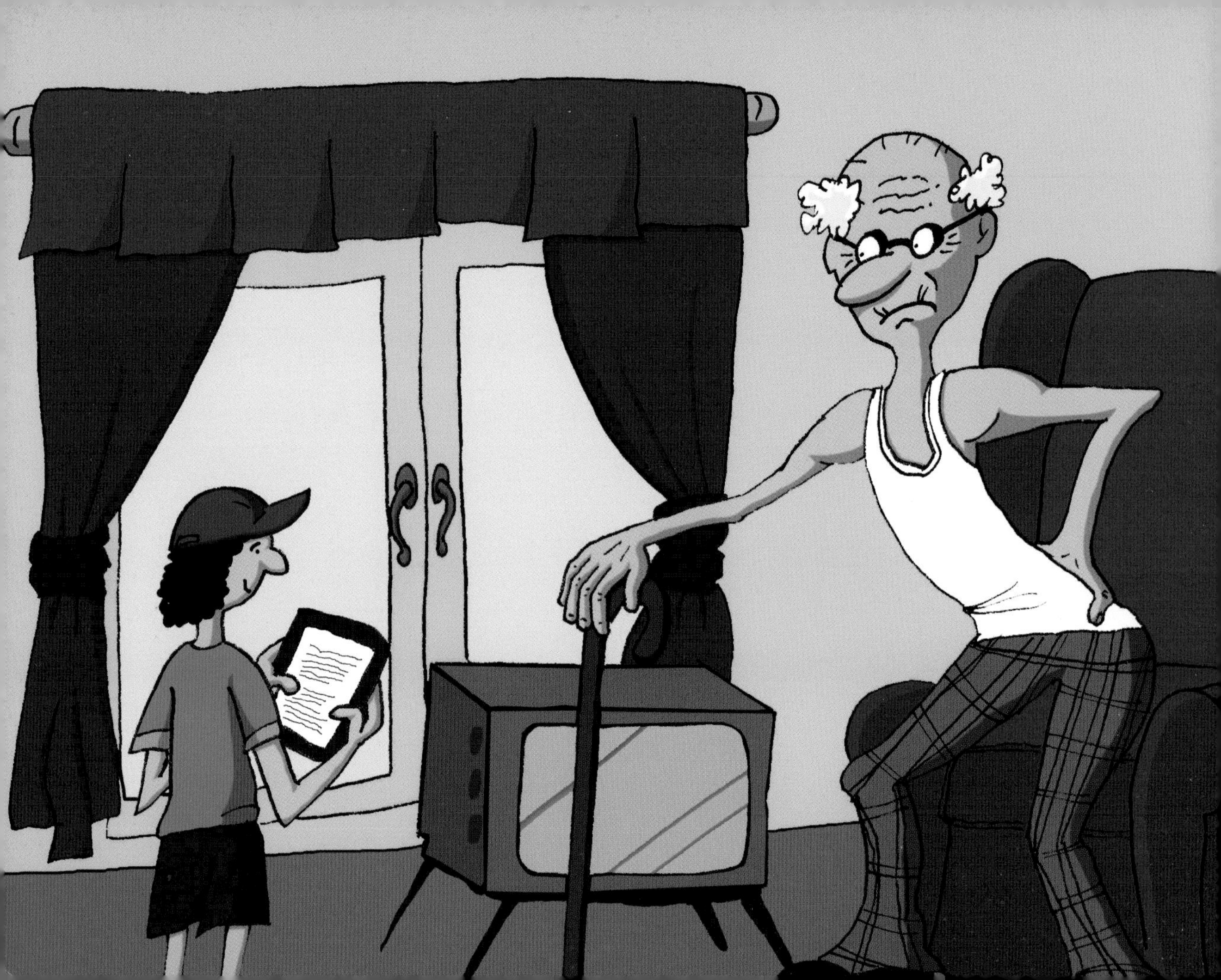

YOU PESTER YOUR TECH-PHOBIC RELATIVES TO SIGN UP.

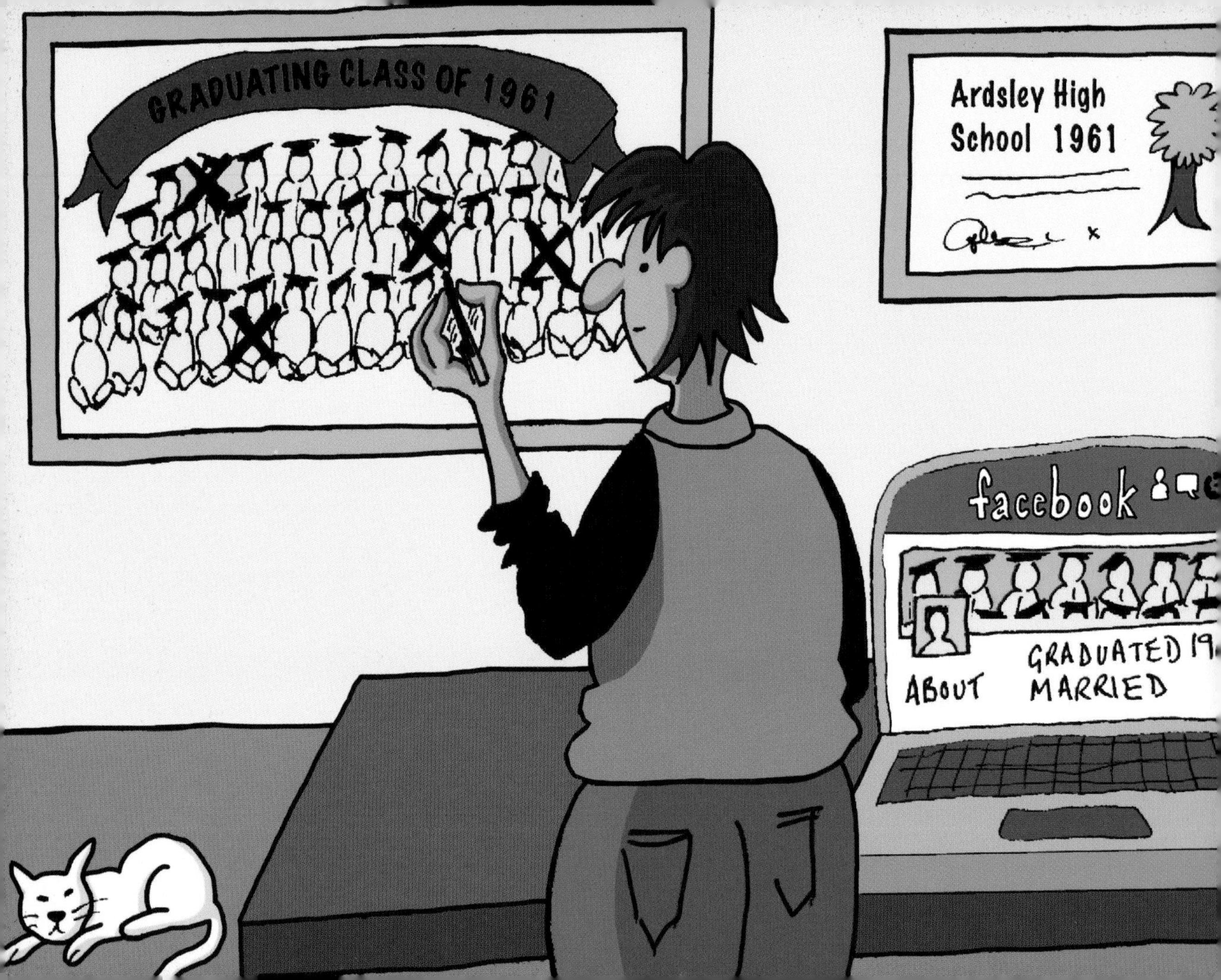
GRADUATING CLASS OF 1961
Ardsley High
School 1961
facebook
GRADUATED 19
ABOUT
MARRIED

STILL SINGLE, YOU STALK YOUR EX-LOVERS TO FIND OUT IF THEY'RE MARRIED, SEPARATED, DIVORCED, OR IF THEY'VE BECOME A PANSEXUAL WITH A FOOT FETISH!

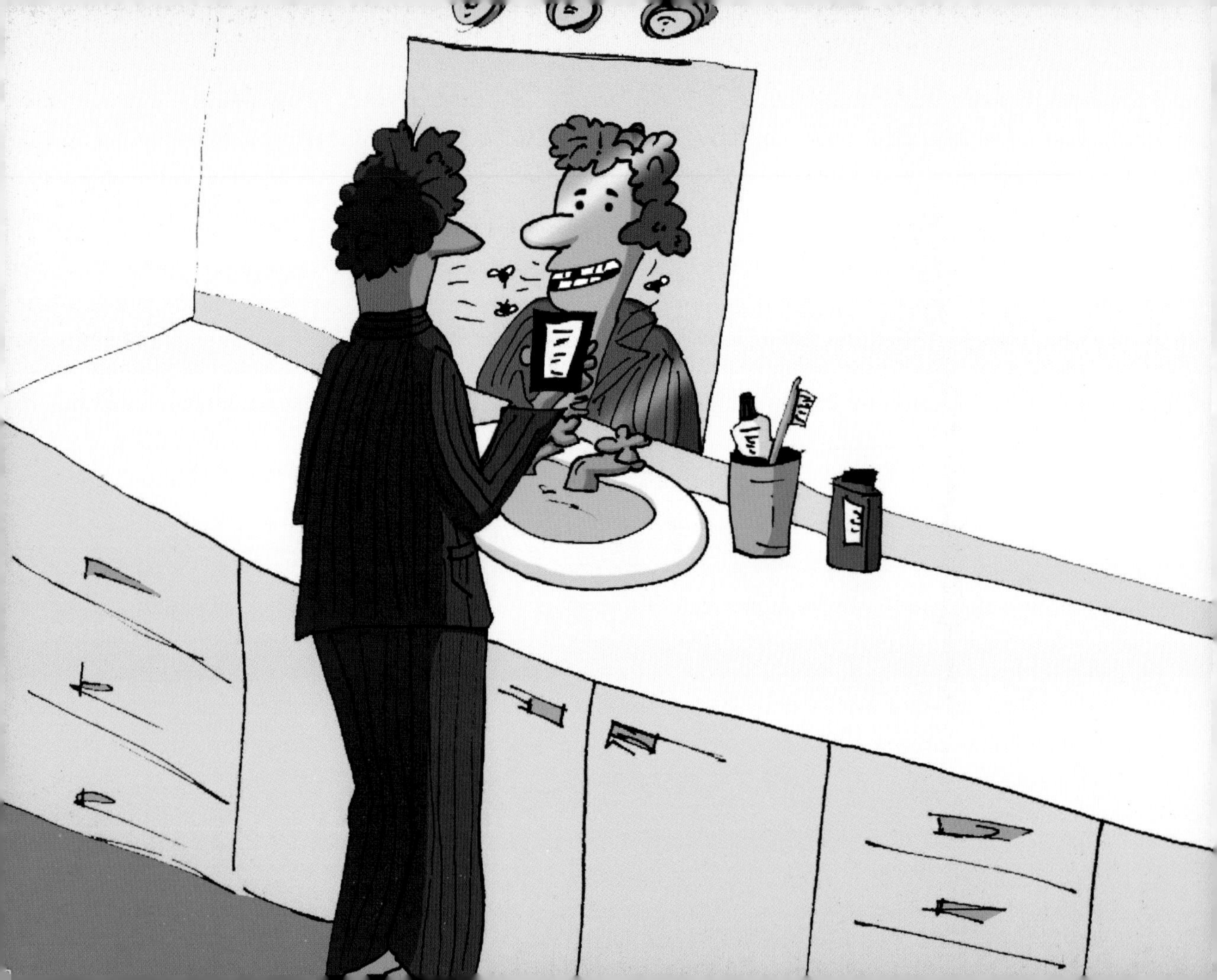

YOU'VE REPLACED YOUR TWICE-
A-DAY RITUAL OF TEETH CLEANING
WITH LOGGING IN TO FACEBOOK.

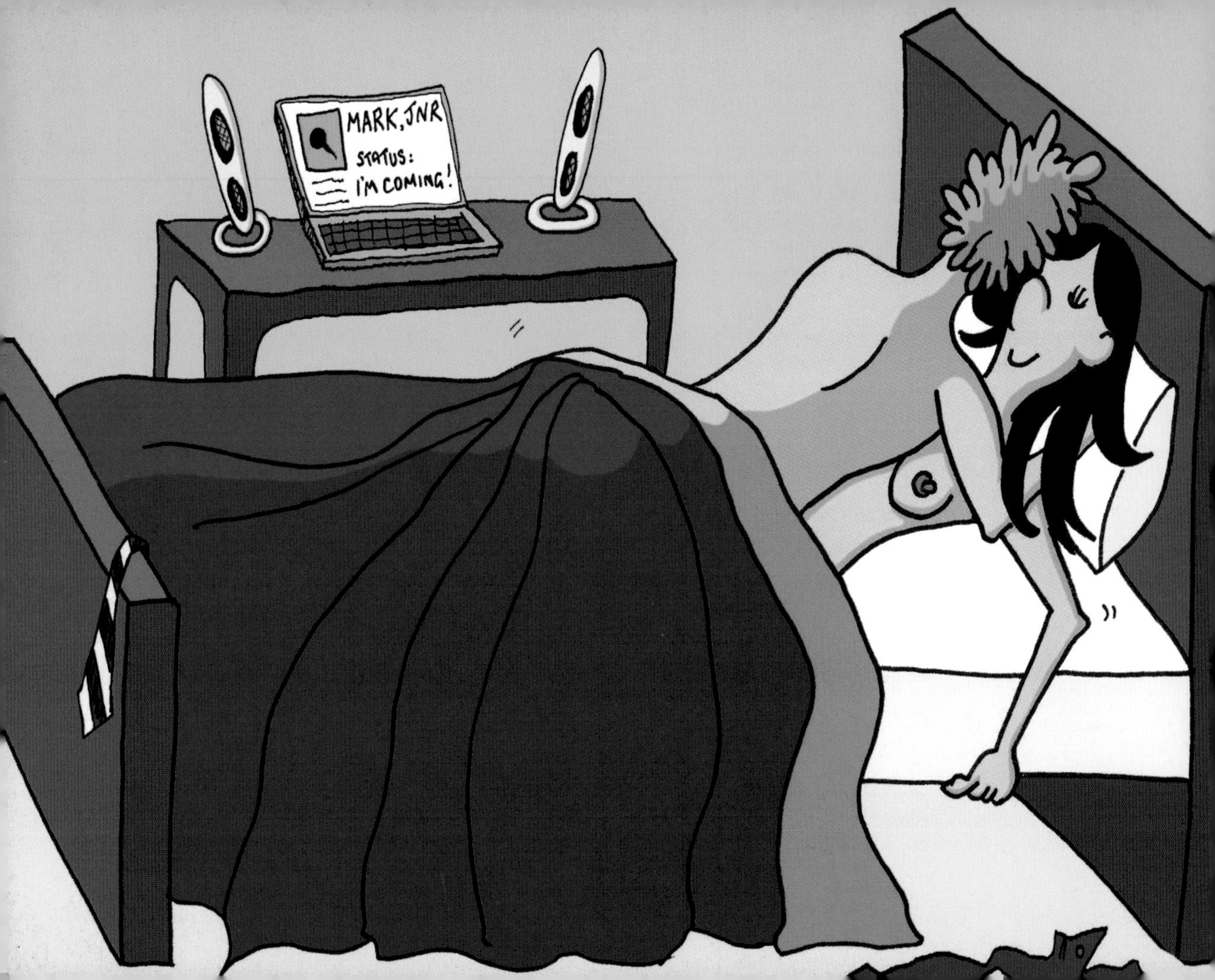
MARK, JNR
STATUS:
I'M COMING!

YOU'VE ALREADY CREATED A PAGE FOR YOUR UNBORN CHILD.

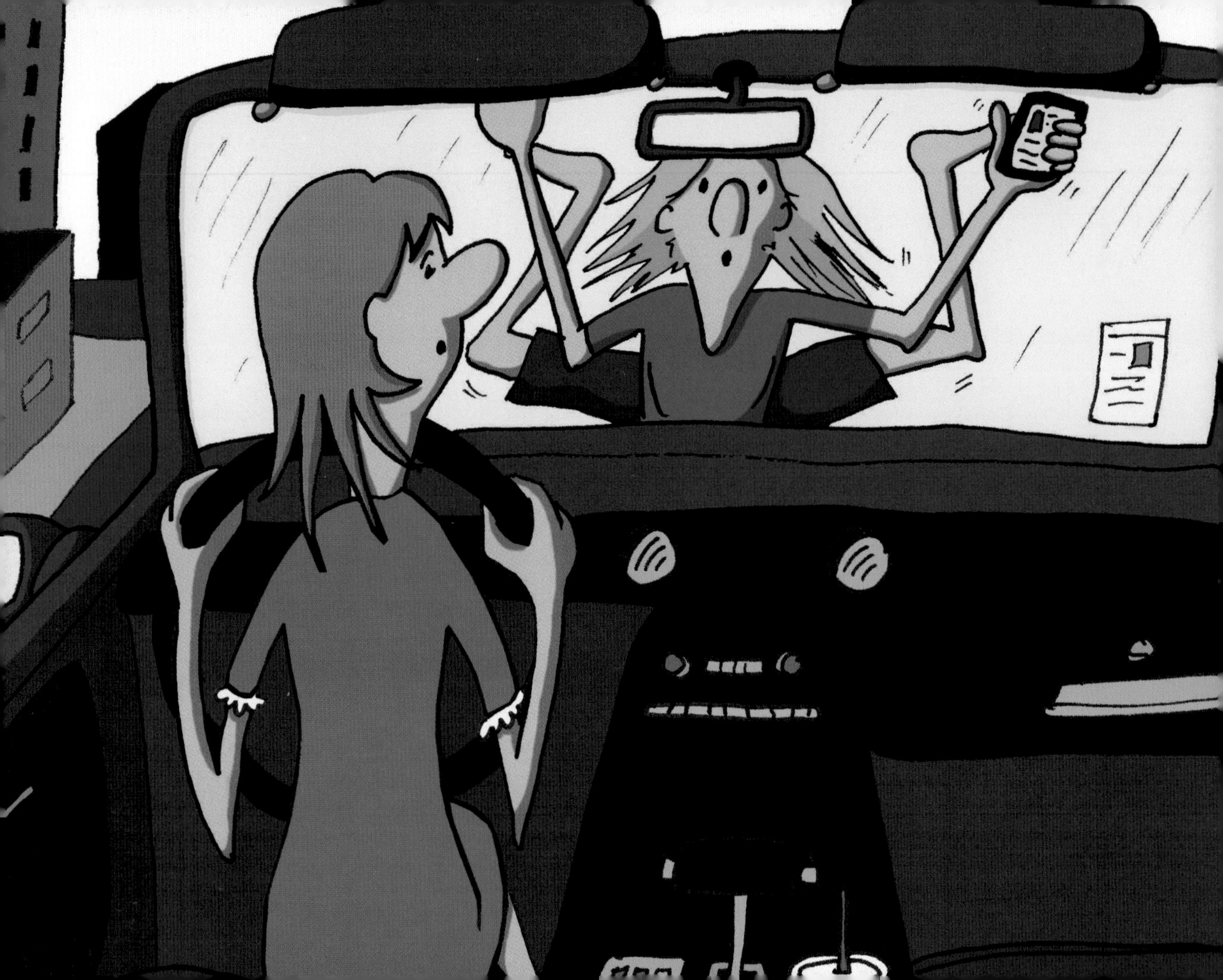

YOU'VE HAD SEVERAL NEAR MISSES CHECKING FACEBOOK WHILE CROSSING THE STREET.

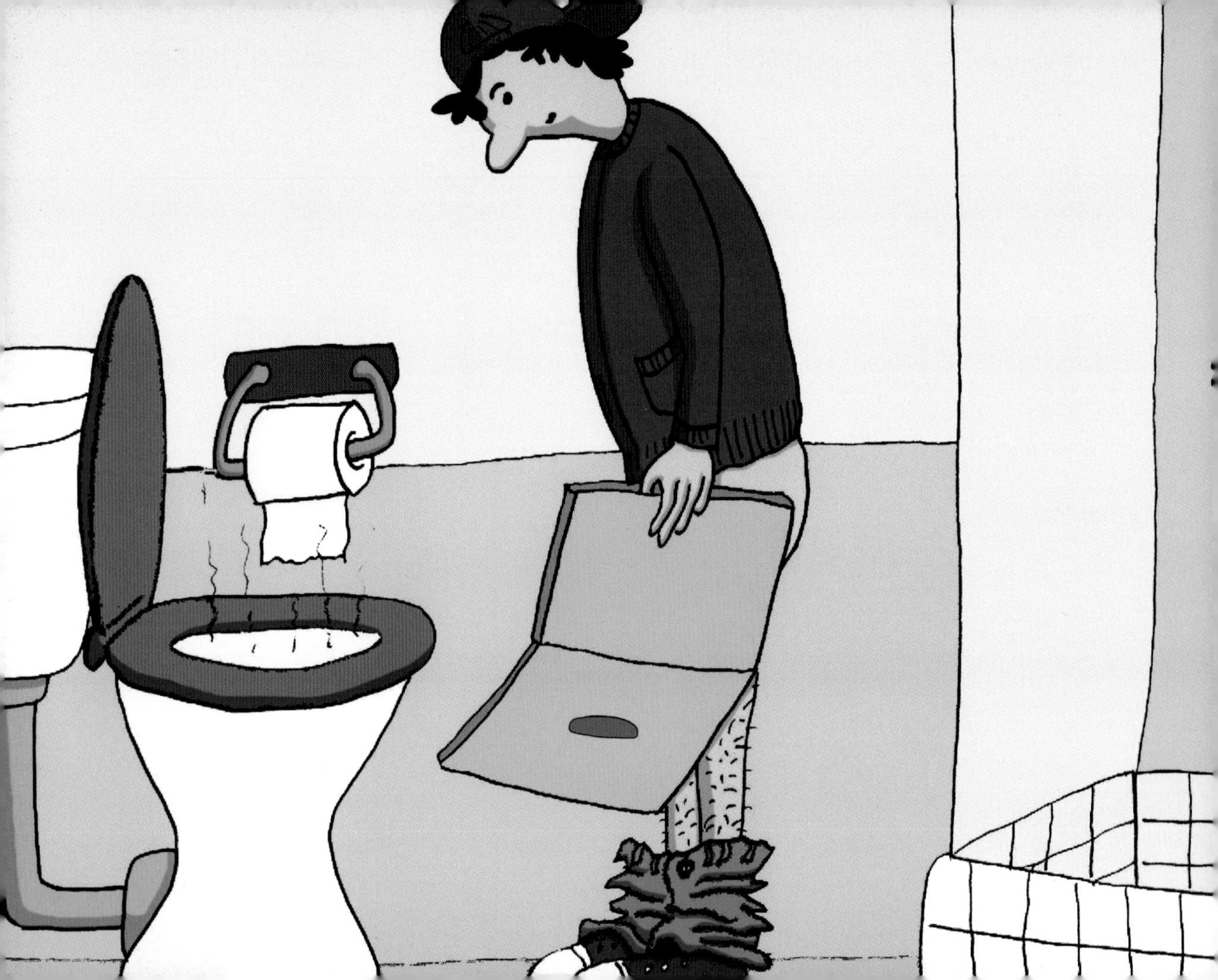

YOU POST MINUTE-BY-MINUTE STATUS UPDATES: "SHOWERING." "EATING INDIAN." "TIRED." "INDIAN FOOD HAS GIVEN ME THE RUNS!"

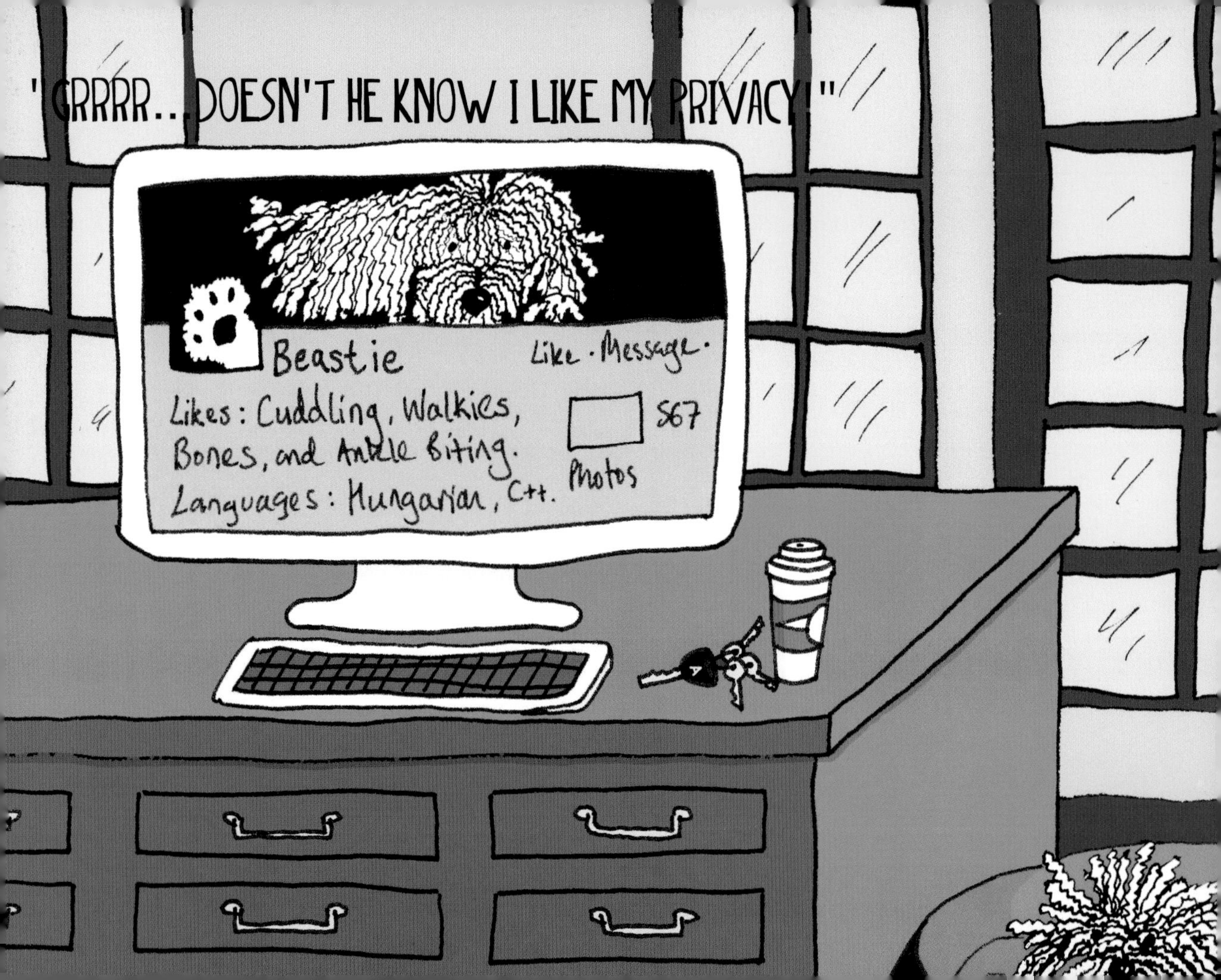
"GRRRR... DOESN'T HE KNOW I LIKE MY PRIVACY!"
Beastie
Like · Message ·
Likes: Cuddling, Walkies, Bones, and Ankle Biting.
567
Photos
Languages: Hungarian, C++.

YOU'VE CREATED A PAGE FOR YOUR IMAGINARY FRIEND, CAT, CAR, OR YOUR DOG.

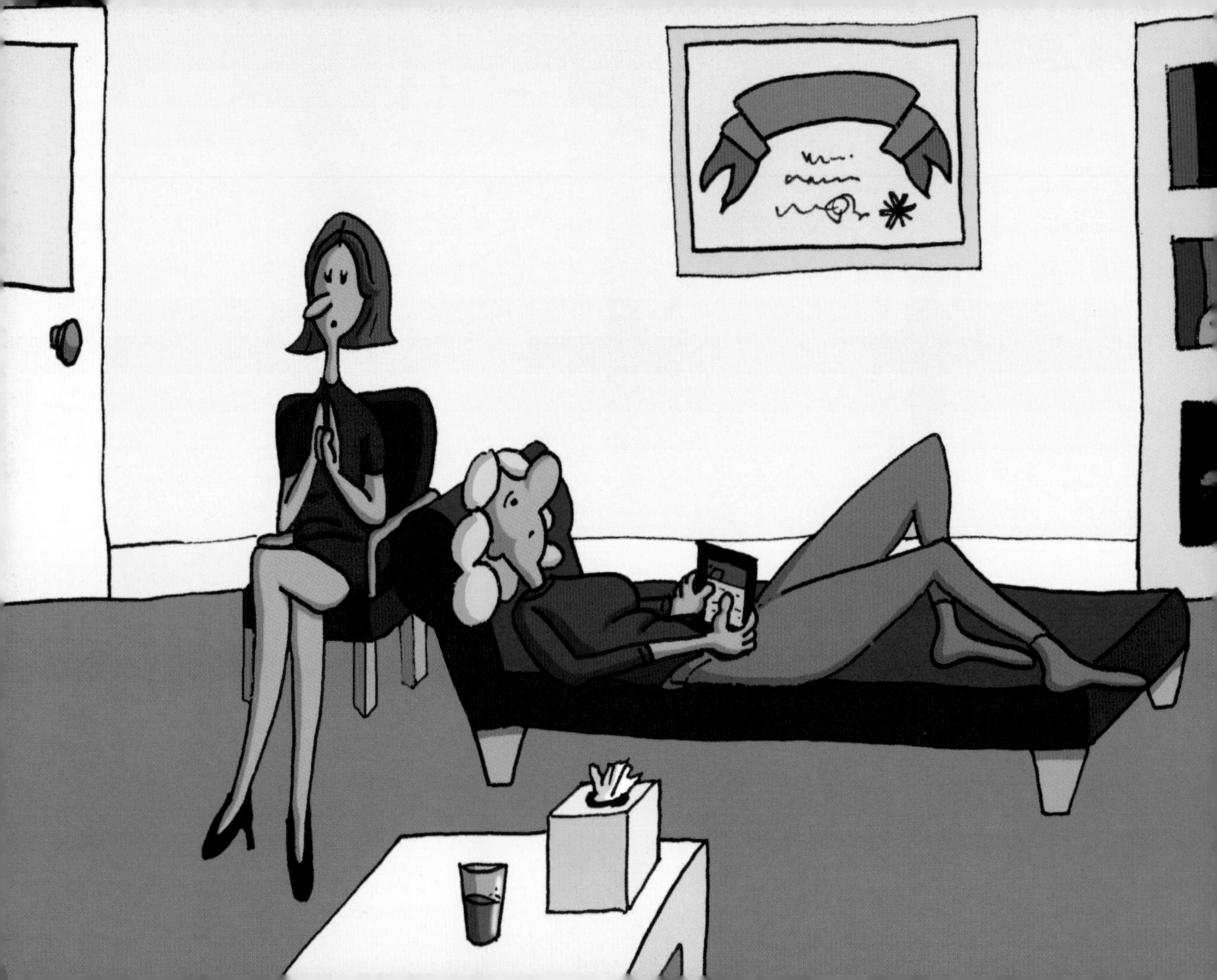

AFTER CHECKING YOUR FORMER BESTIE'S PROFILE PAGE— THE EVER-SO-SUCCESSFUL MARRIED BITCH WITH THREE MODEL PERFECT CHILDREN — YOU HAVE TO VISIT YOUR THERAPIST.

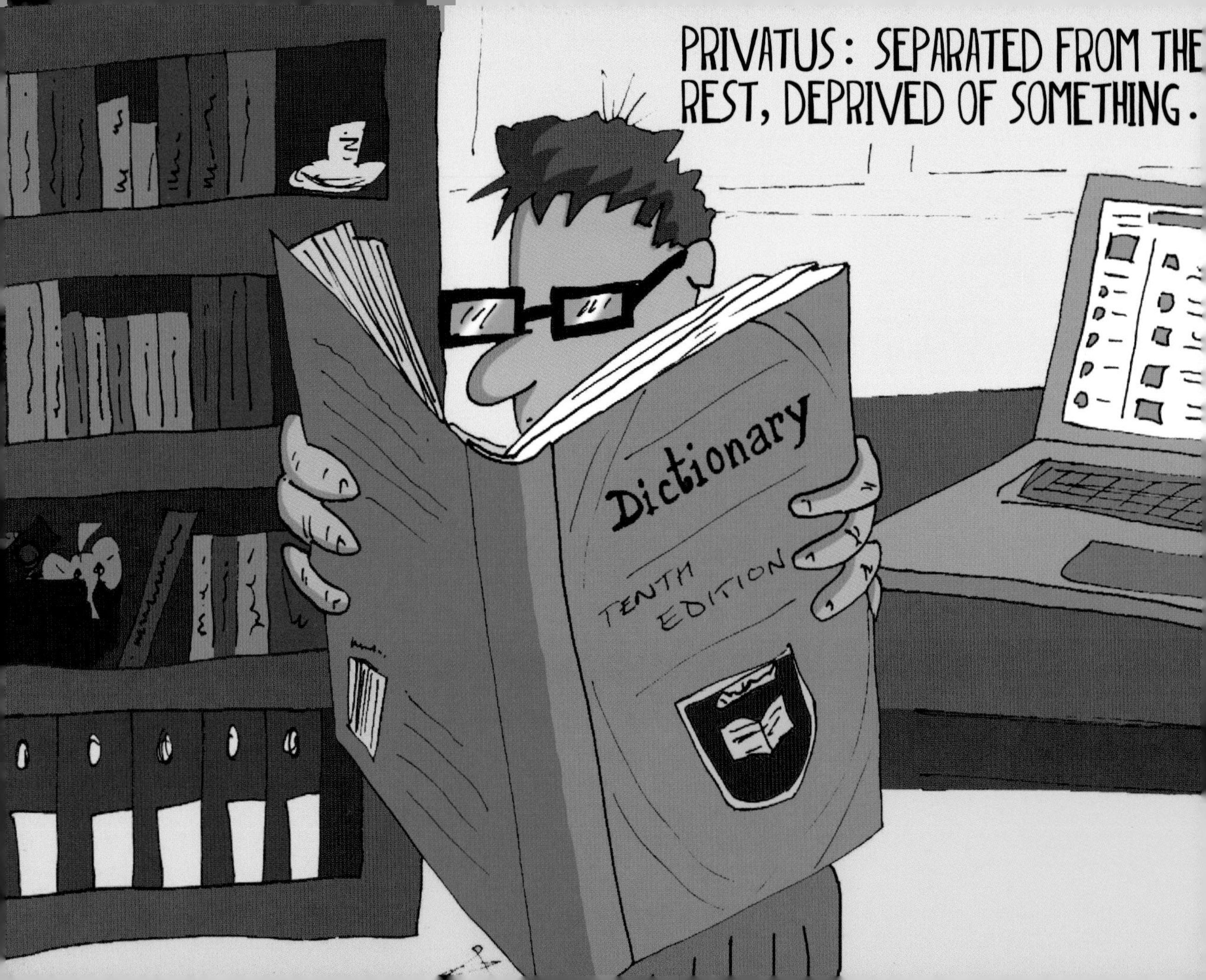
PRIVATUS: SEPARATED FROM THE REST, DEPRIVED OF SOMETHING.
Dictionary
TENTH EDITION

YOU HAVE NO IDEA WHERE THE PRIVACY SETTINGS ARE ON YOUR ACCOUNT.

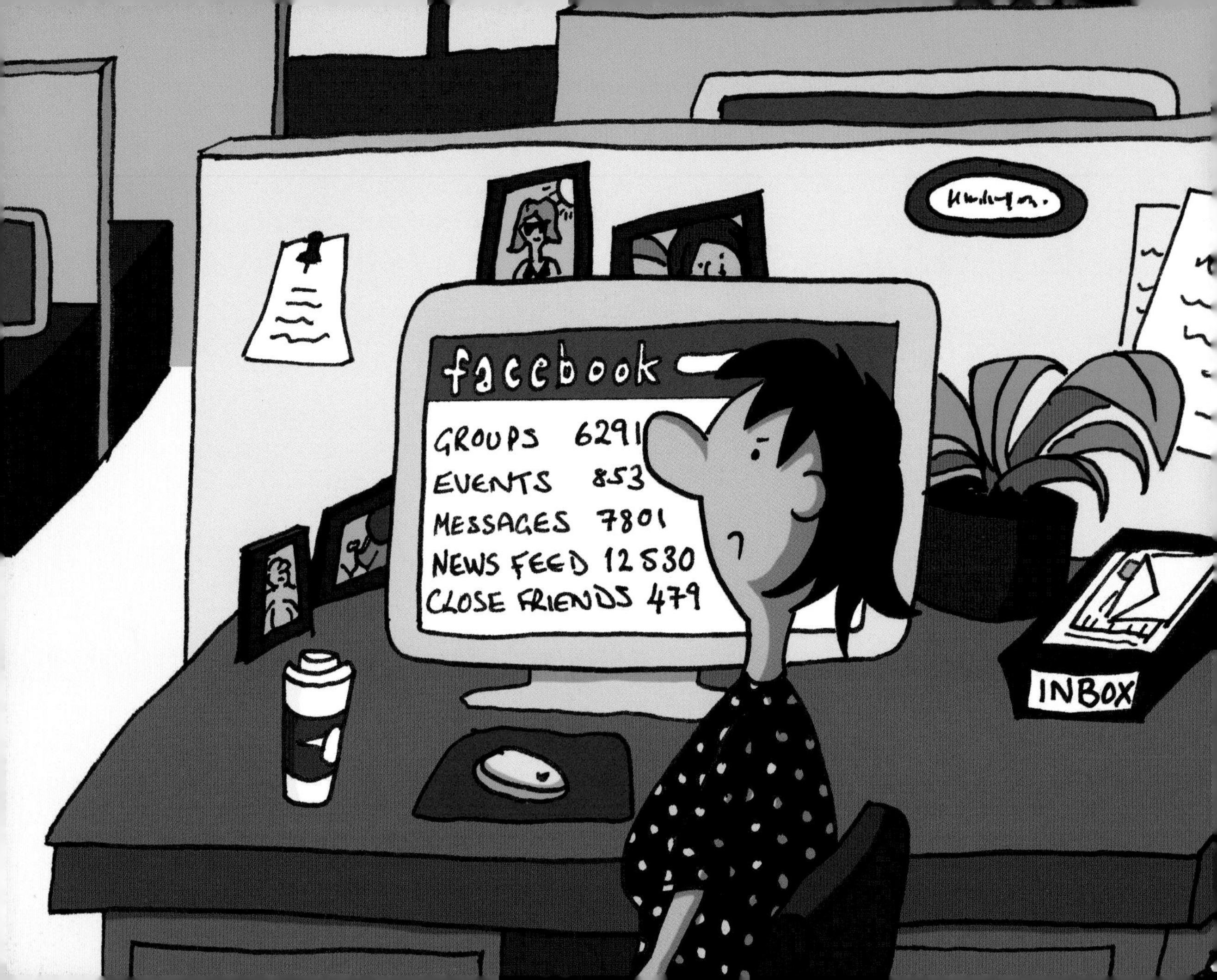
facebook
GROUPS 6291
EVENTS 853
MESSAGES 7801
NEWS FEED 12530
CLOSE FRIENDS 479
INBOX

YOU'VE SIGNED UP TO SOOO MANY PAGES, YOU'RE OVERWHELMED BY YOUR INBOX.

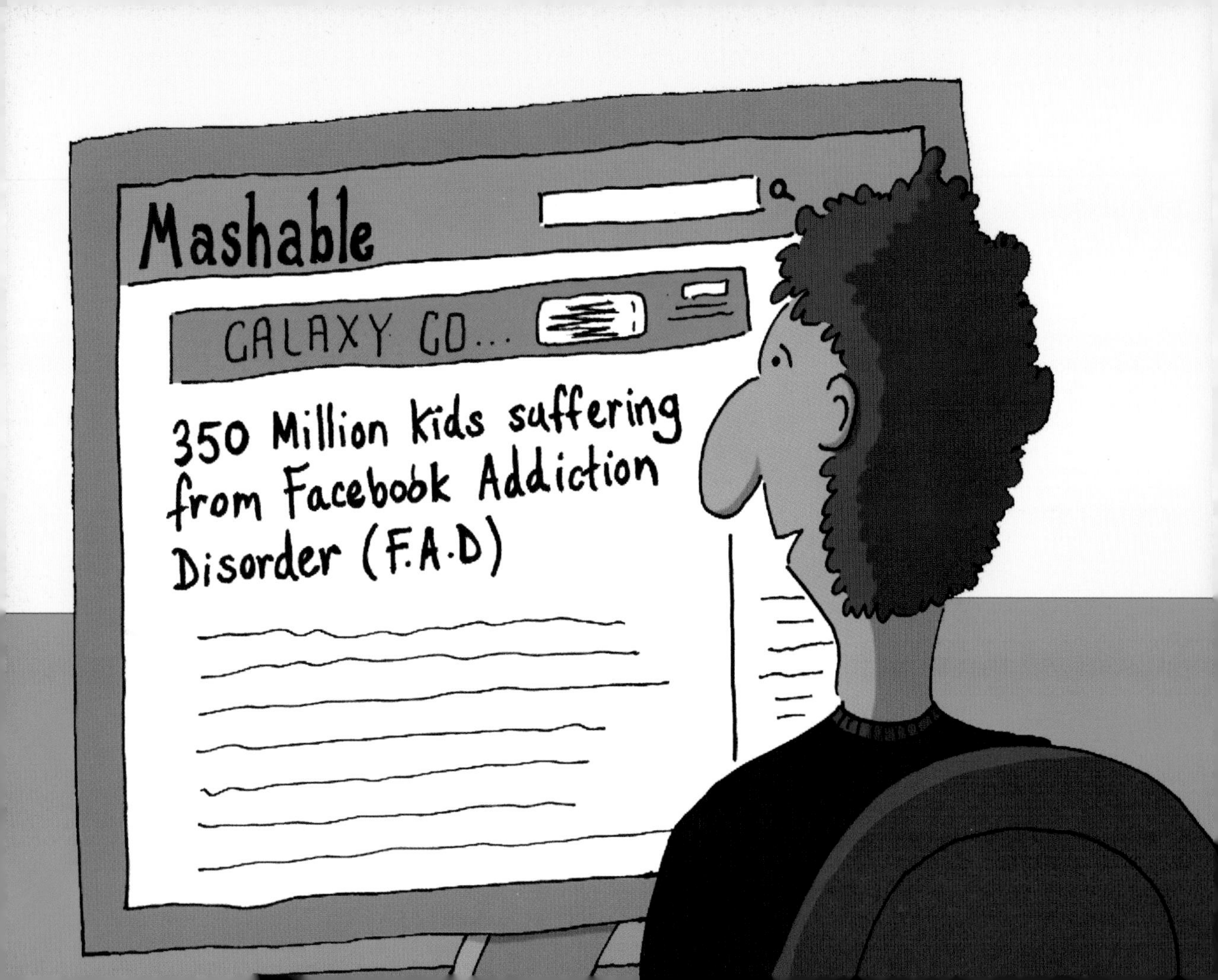
Mashable
GALAXY GO...
350 Million kids suffering from Facebook Addiction Disorder (F.A.D)

FOR SOME REASON PEOPLE KEEP SENDING YOU LINKS TO ARTICLES ON FACEBOOK ADDICTION DISORDER (F.A.D.).

DEP | HONG KONG ARR. SOUVLAKISTAN 6:57
DEP | NEW YORK ARR. SOUVLAKISTAN 7:15
DEP | LONDON ARR. SOUVLAKISTAN 7:33
DEP | LOS ANGELES ARR. SOUVLAKISTAN 7:52
EXIT
ertz

YOU'VE FOUND AND BEFRIENDED SOME DISTANT RELATIVES IN SOUVLAKISTAN — AND ARRANGED TO VISIT.

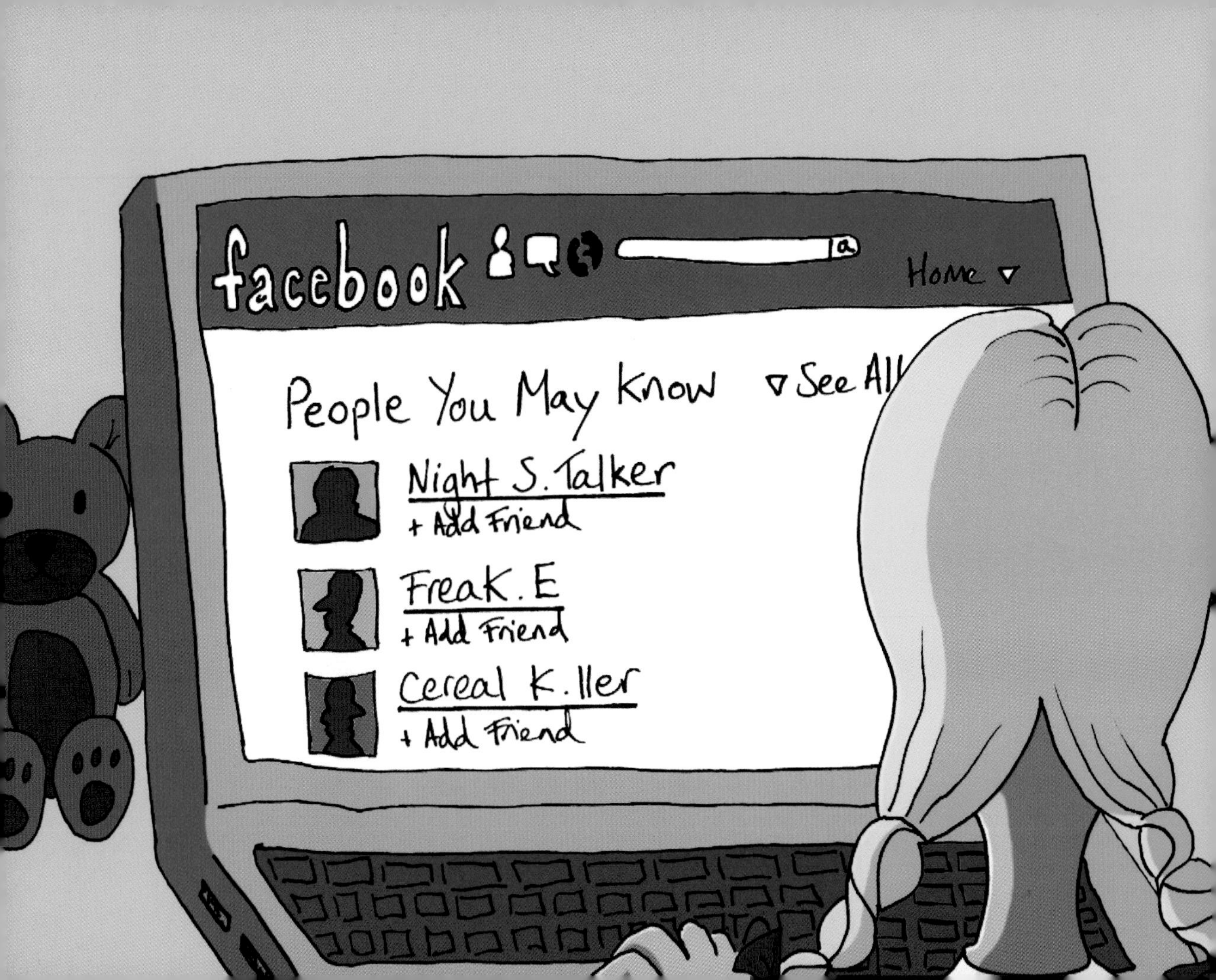
facebook
Home
People You May Know
See All
Night S. Talker
+ Add Friend
Freak. E
+ Add Friend
Cereal K. ller
+ Add Friend

YOU GLEEFULLY SEND FRIEND REQUESTS TO EVERYONE IN THE "PEOPLE YOU MAY KNOW" SECTION.

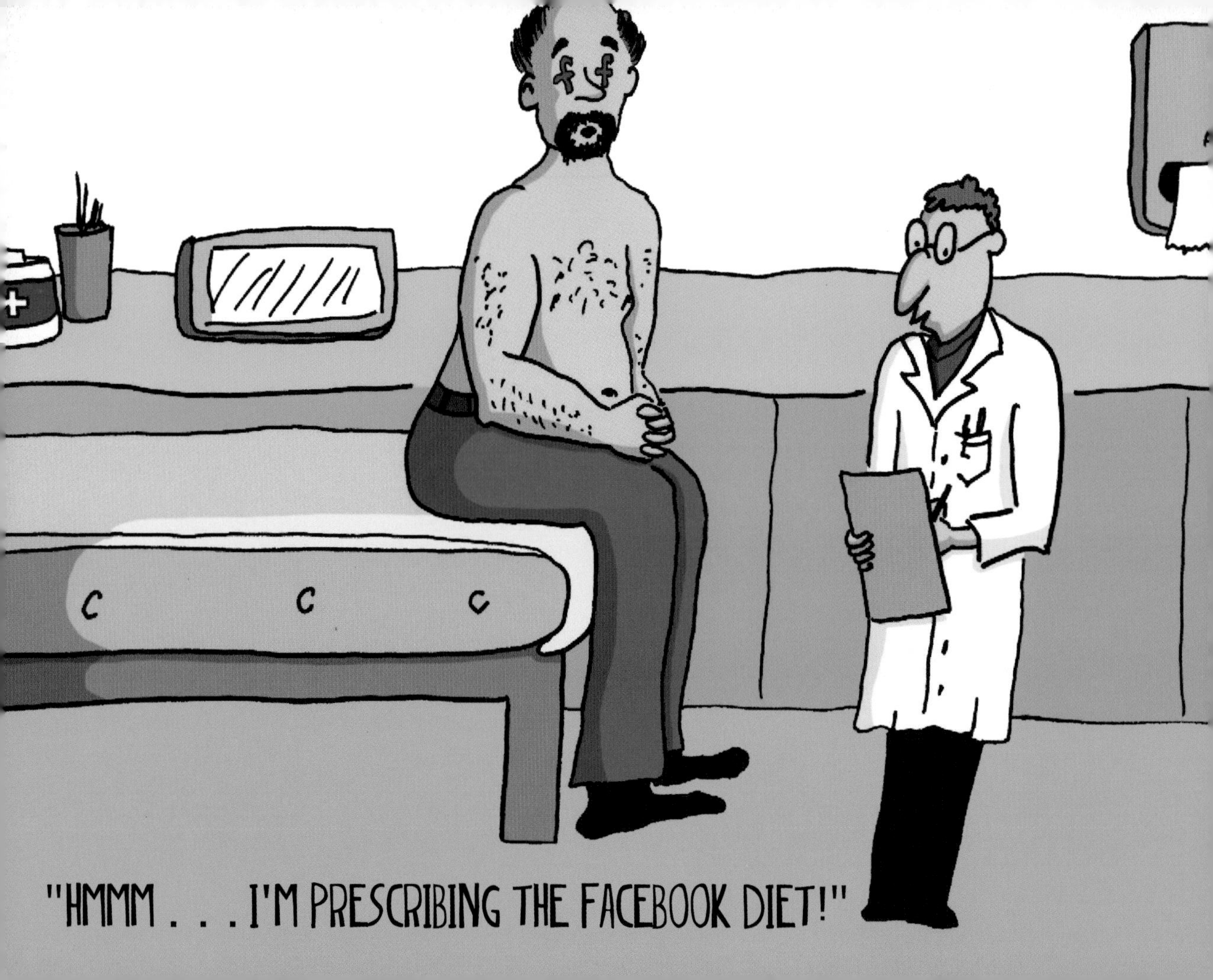

"HMMM . . . I'M PRESCRIBING THE FACEBOOK DIET!"

YOU'VE GOT FACE ACHE FROM SPENDING WAAAAAAY TOO MUCH TIME ON FACEBOOK.

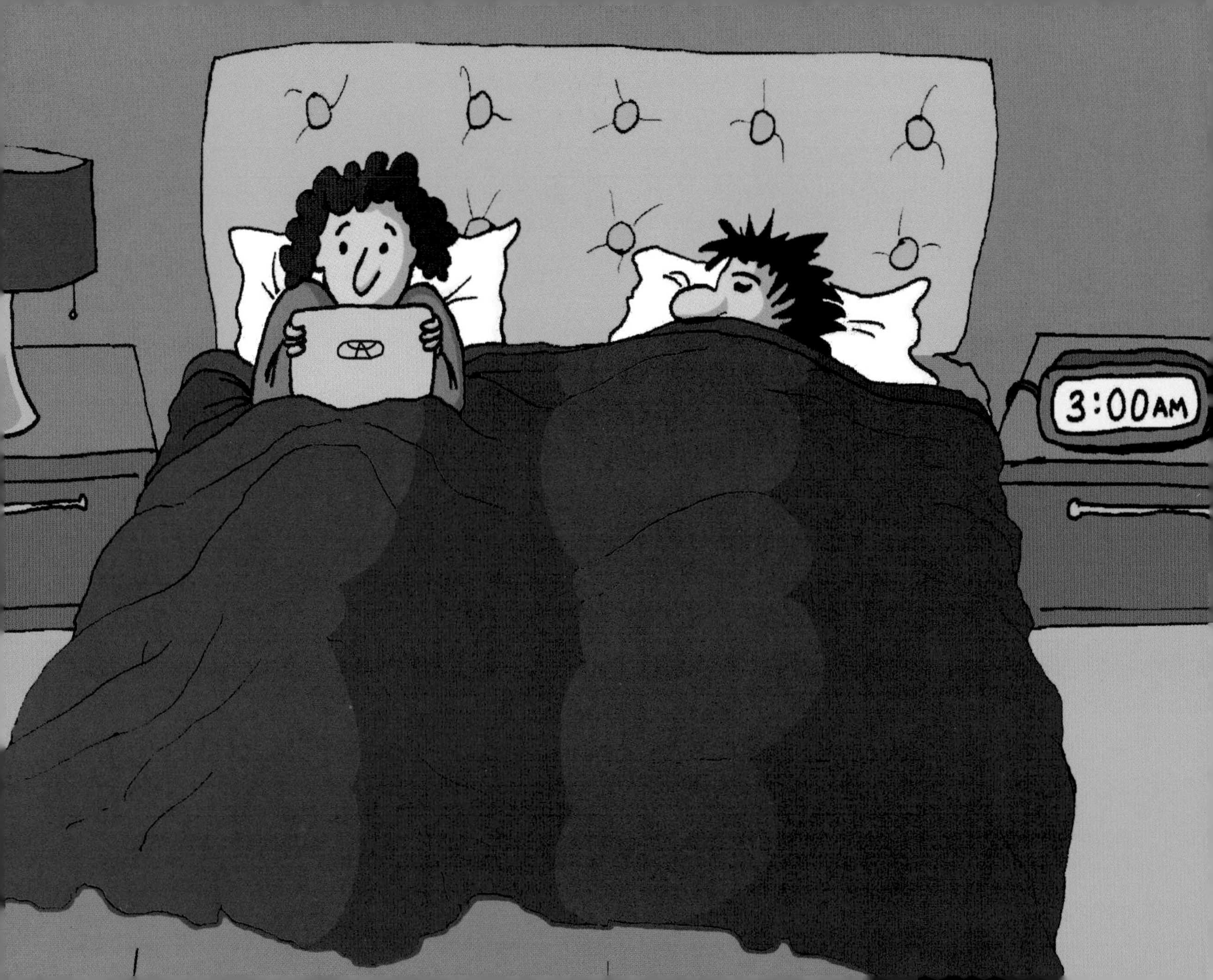
3:00AM

YOU FREQUENTLY STAY UP LATE STALKING YOUR FRIENDS, OR POSTING YOUTUBE VIDEOS OF STUPIDLY CUTE KITTENS.

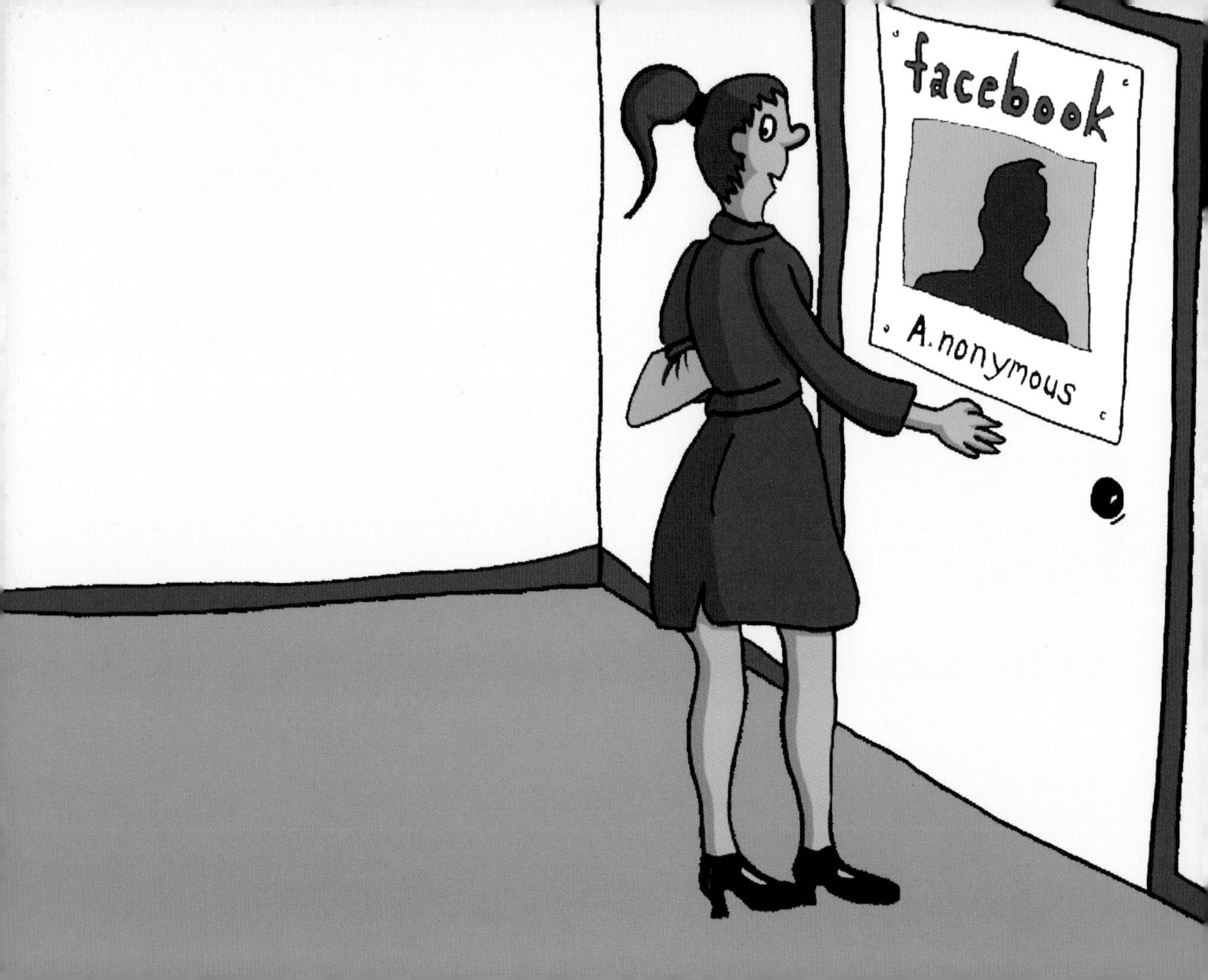
facebook
A.nonymous

YOUR FRIENDS KEEP JOKING THAT YOU SHOULD JOIN A FACEBOOK ANONYMOUS GROUP.

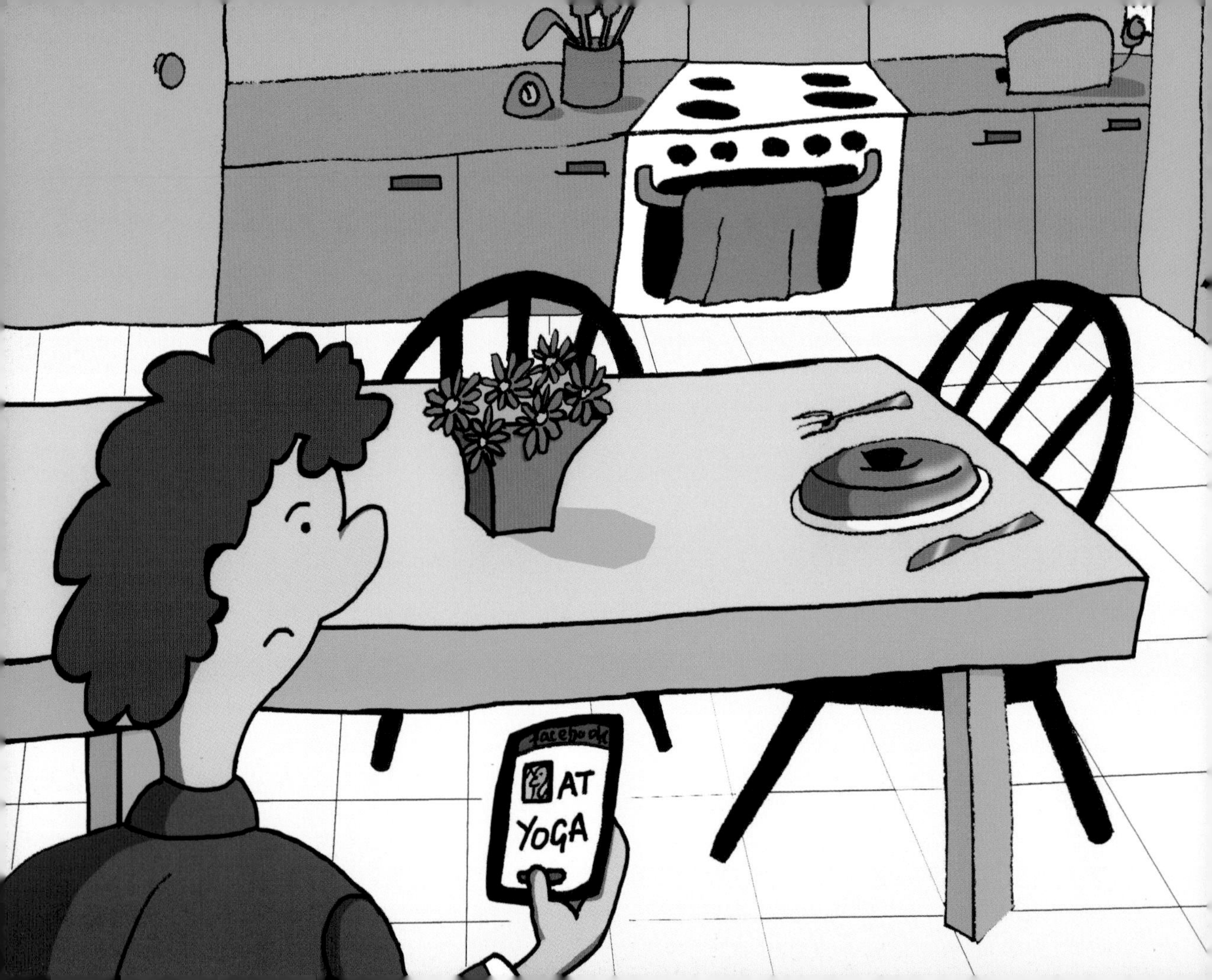
facebook
AT
YOGA

YOUR LOVED ONES HAVE TO CHECK YOUR STATUS TO FIND OUT WHERE YOU'VE GONE.

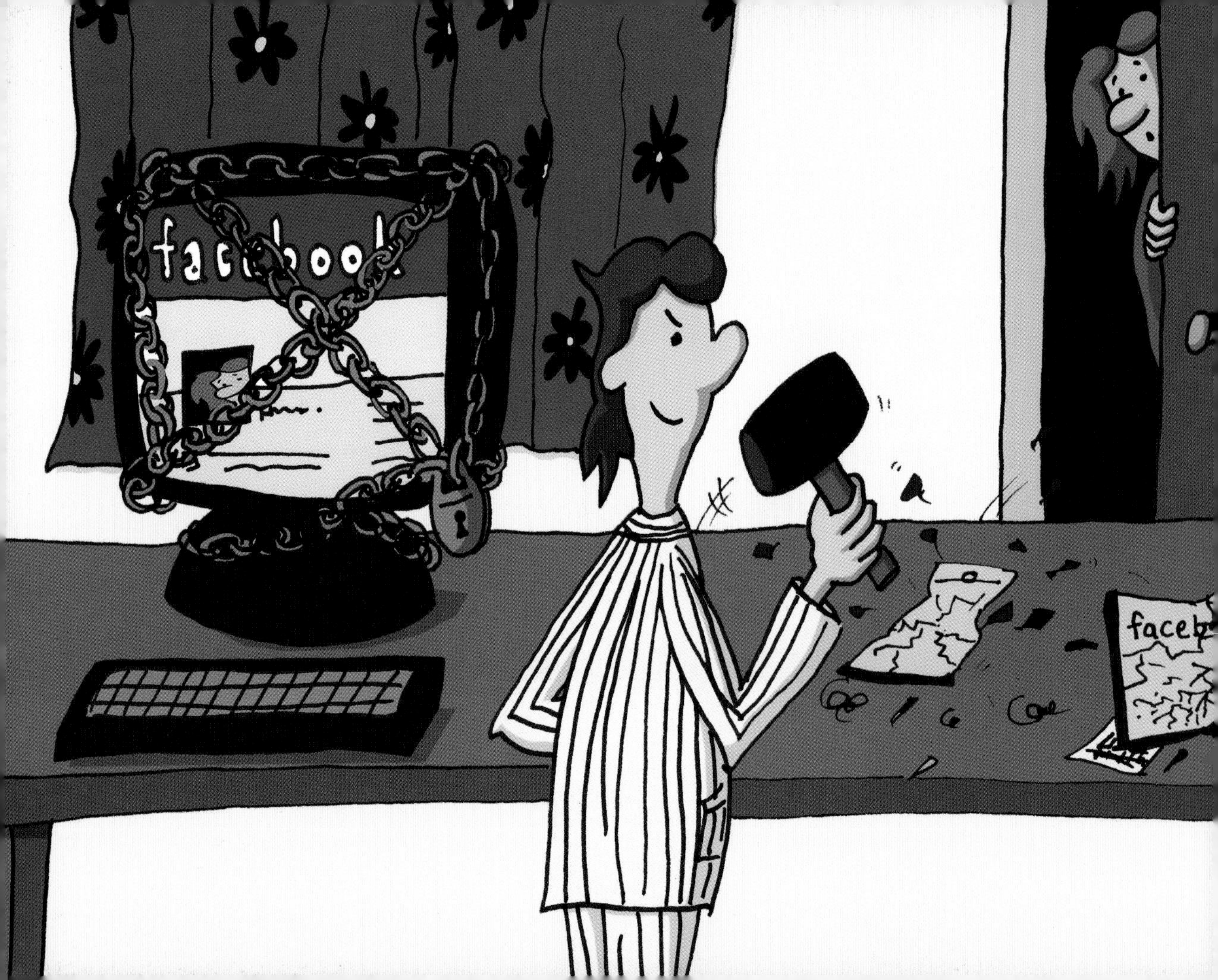
facebook
faceb

YOUR PARTNER ANGRILY CLAIMS THEY'VE BECOME A FACEBOOK WIDOW.

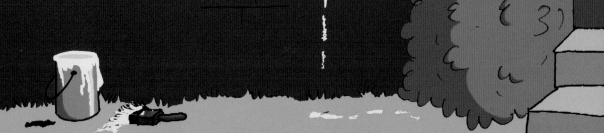

PARTY AT MY PLACE THIS WEEKEND

YOU PHONE YOUR FRIEND TO ASK:
"DID YOU SEE WHAT I WROTE ON
YOUR WALL TODAY?"

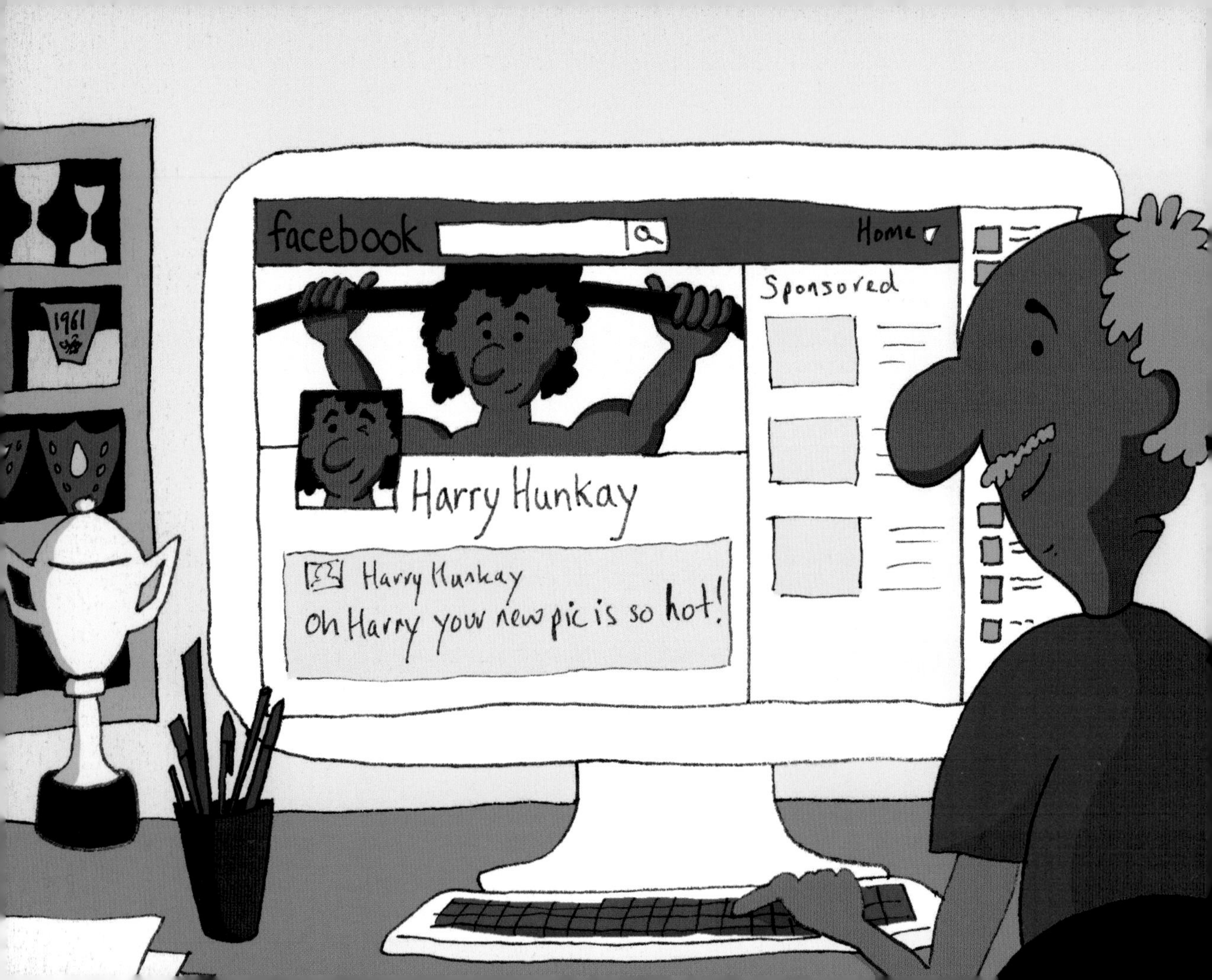

facebook
Home
Sponsored
Harry Hunkay
Harry Hunkay
Oh Harry your new pic is so hot!
1961

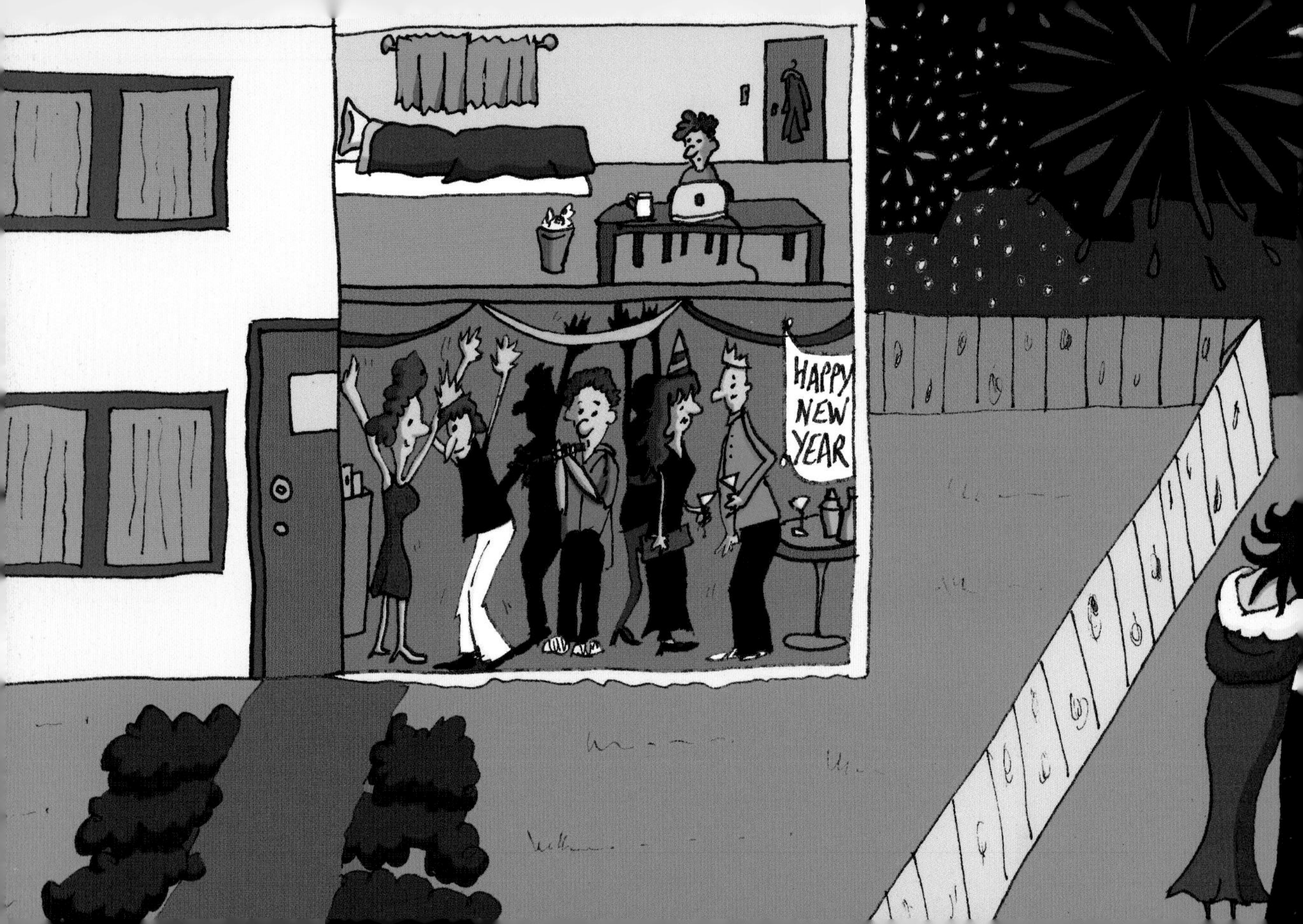
HAPPY NEW YEAR

YOU NO LONGER PARTICIPATE IN FACE-TO-FACE SOCIAL INTERACTION PERIOD.

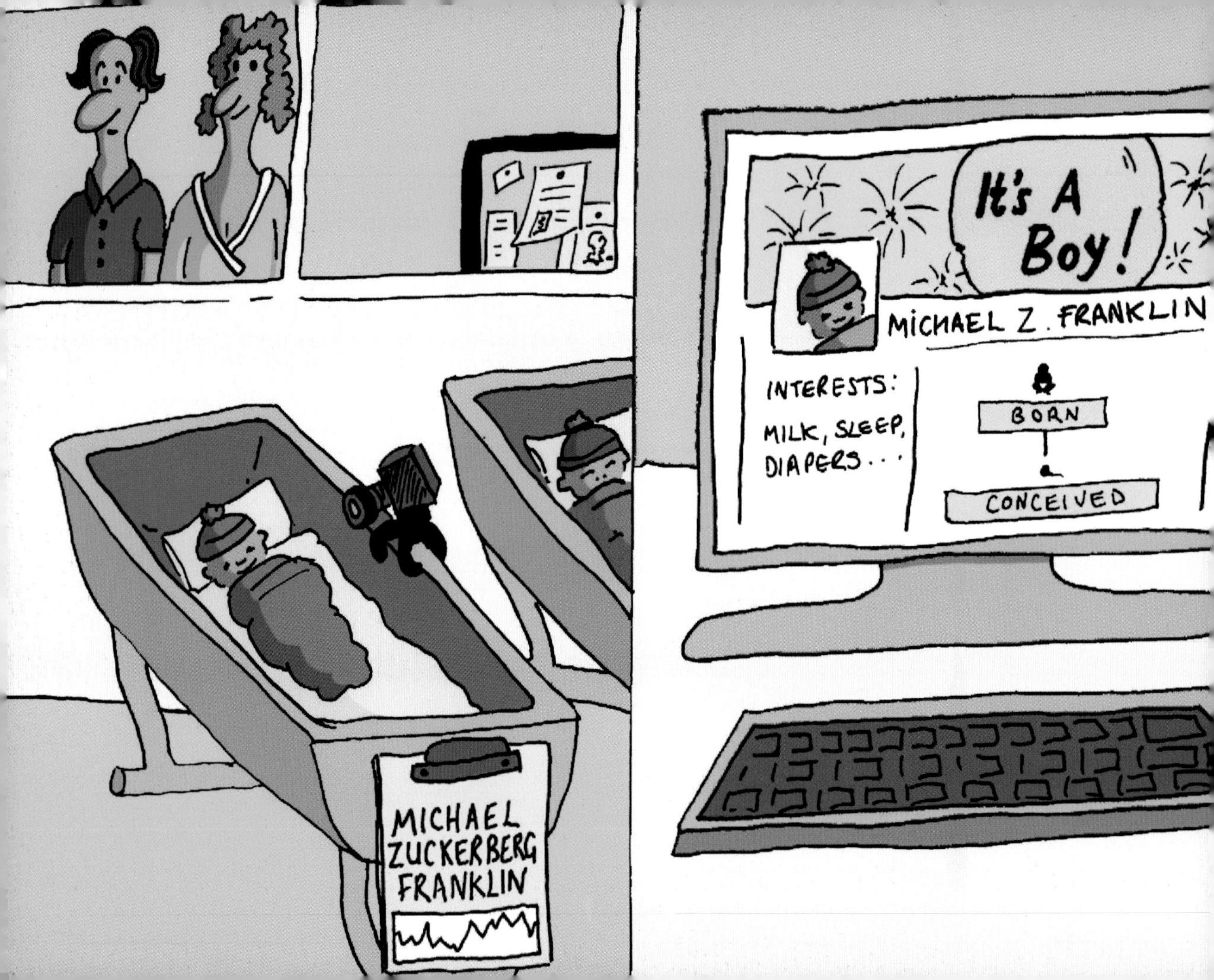
MICHAEL ZUCKERBERG FRANKLIN
It's A Boy!
MICHAEL Z. FRANKLIN
INTERESTS:
MILK, SLEEP, DIAPERS...
BORN
CONCEIVED

YOU'VE DECIDED TO NAME YOUR FIRST-BORN SON MARK OR GIVE YOUR SECOND CHILD ZUCKERBERG AS A MIDDLE NAME.

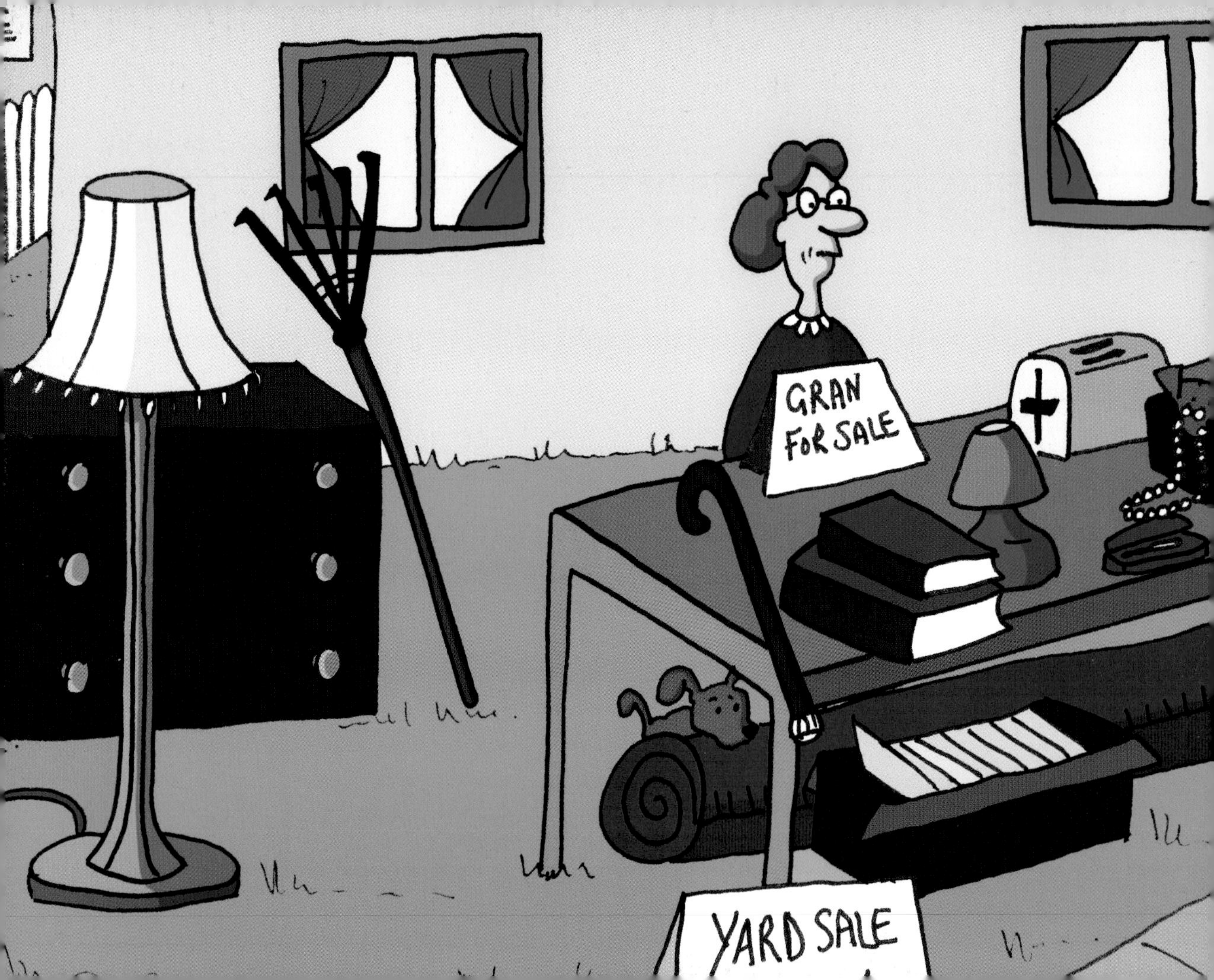
GRAN FOR SALE
YARD SALE

YOU'VE SOLD EVERYTHING SO YOU CAN BUY FACEBOOK STOCK.

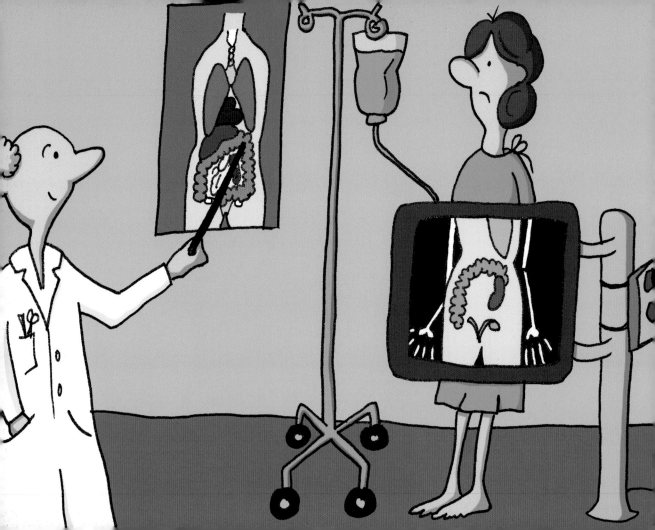

YOU GOT A BIT CARRIED AWAY WHEN YOU REGISTERED AS AN ORGAN DONOR ON YOUR TIMELINE.

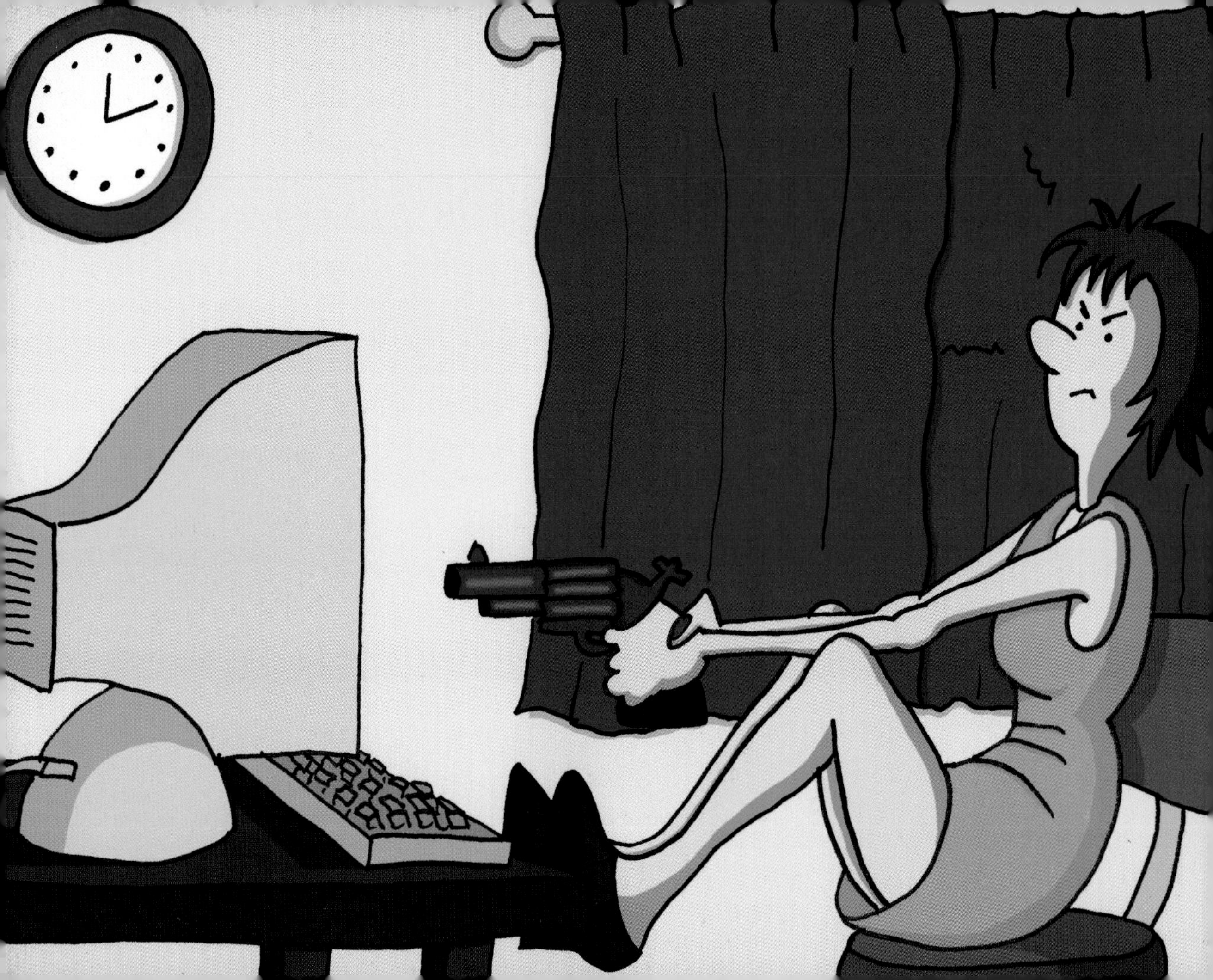

YOU'VE HAD A FACE-OFF WITH FACEBOOK.

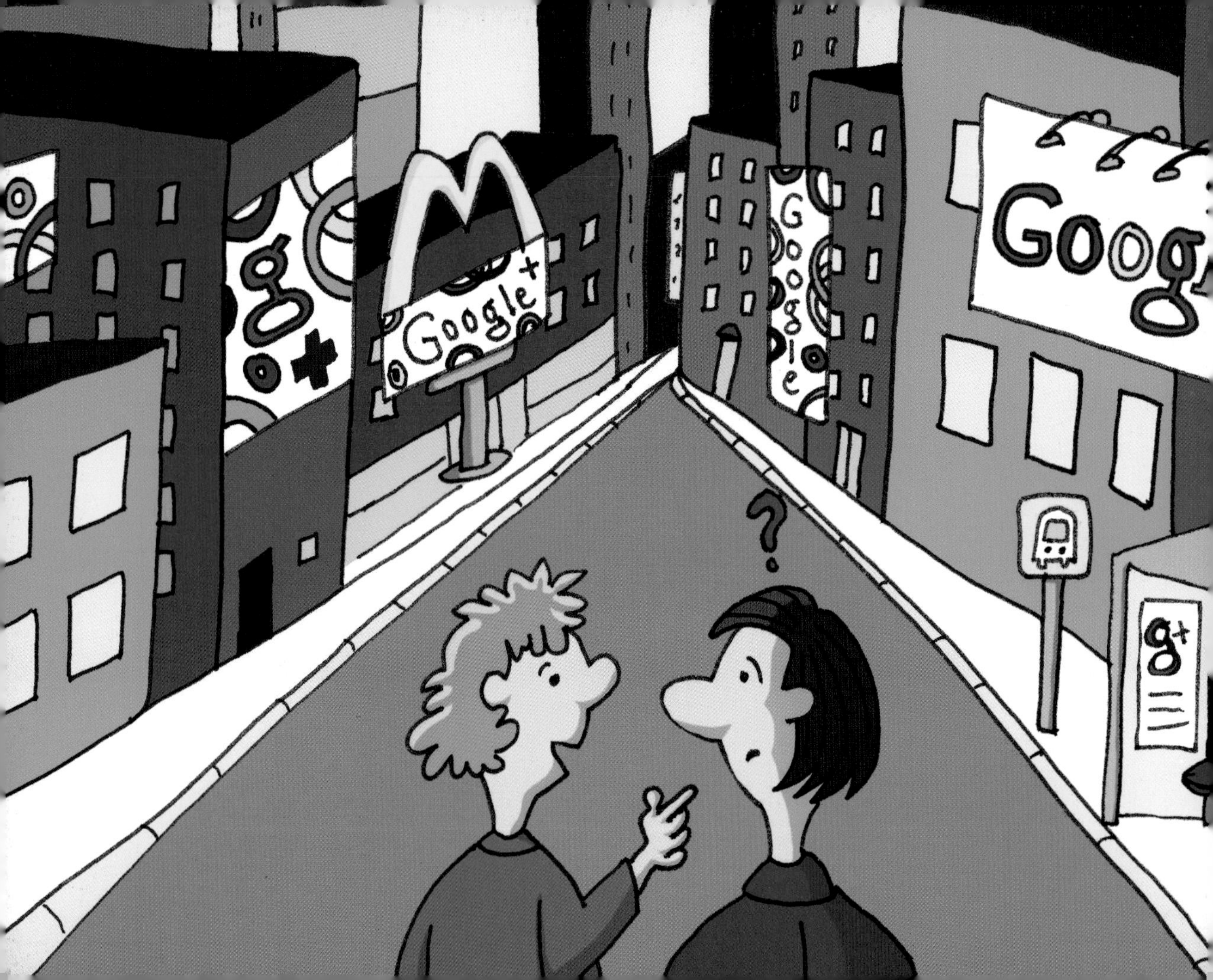
Google+
Google
Goog

YOU REALLY HAVE NO IDEA WHAT GOOGLE+ OR CIRCLES ARE.

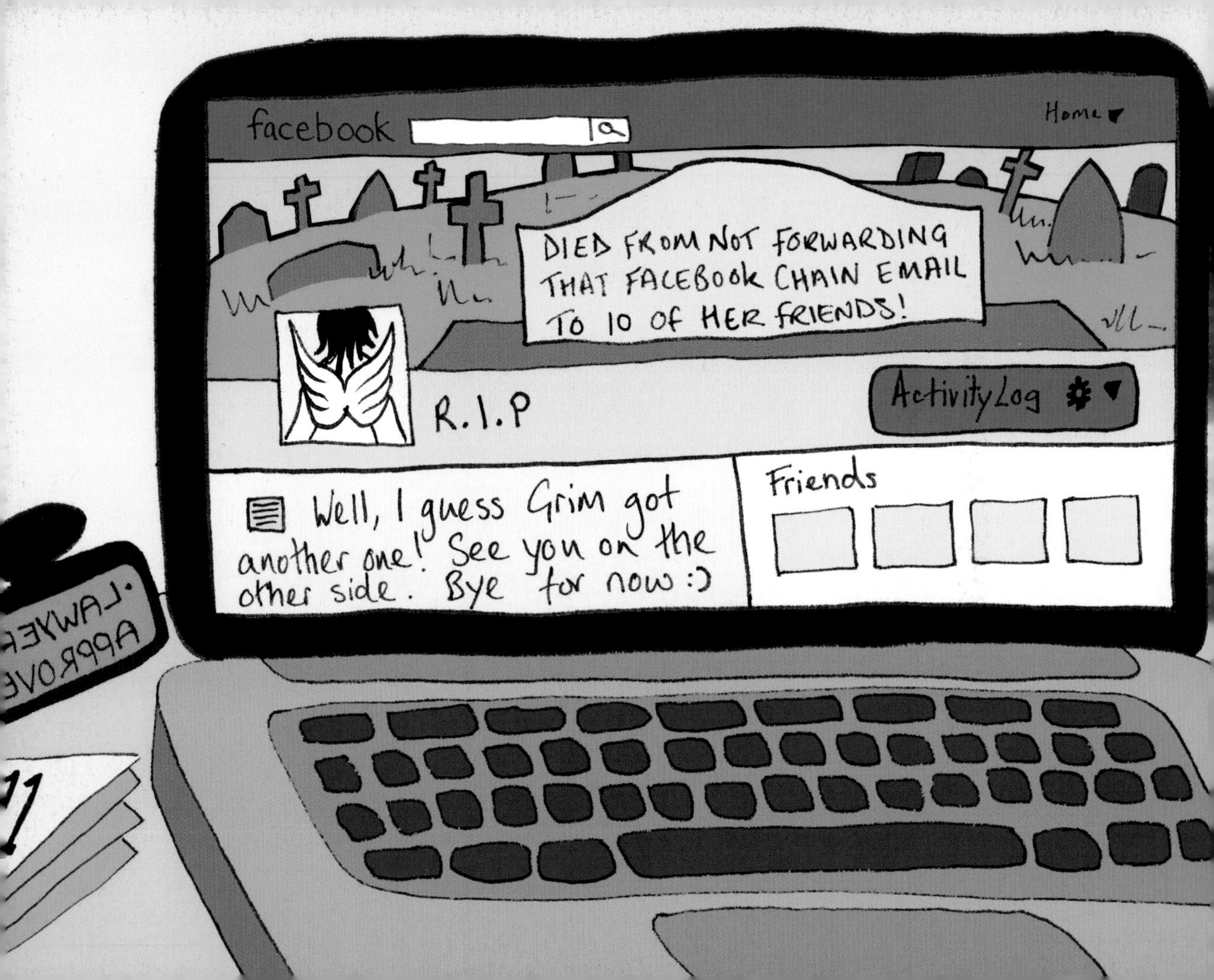
facebook
Home
DIED FROM NOT FORWARDING THAT FACEBOOK CHAIN EMAIL TO 10 OF HER FRIENDS!
R.I.P
Activity Log
Well, I guess Grim got another one! See you on the other side. Bye for now :)
Friends

YOU'VE LEFT YOUR PASSWORD AND AN OBITUARY STATUS UPDATE IN YOUR WILL.

IF YOU'VE FALLEN DEEPLY INTO THE TECHNOLOGY RABBIT HOLE THAT IS FACEBOOK, THEN MAYBE IT'S TIME TO UNPLUG AND TAKE A DIGITAL DETOX. WE PRESCRIBE . . .

THE FACEBOOK DIET

IT'S TIME TO UNPLUG!

CLOSE YOUR FACEBOOK ACCOUNT... DUH.

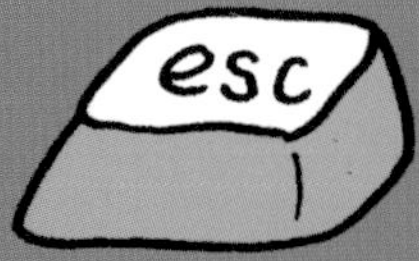
esc

TAKE A DIGITAL DETOX!

START OR JOIN A CLUB. ONE WITH REAL LIVE HUMAN INTERACTION, SPIT, WARTS, BAD BREATH, AND ALL!

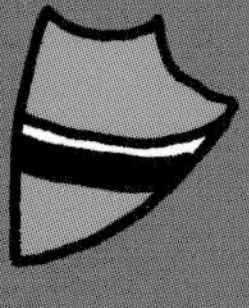

IT'S TIME TO UNPLUG!

FALL IN LOVE.

TAKE A DIGITAL DETOX!

Spend a year living with an Amazonian tribe deep in the jungle.

TAKE UP KNITTING OR BIRD WATCHING, BUT NOT THE ANGRY ONES.

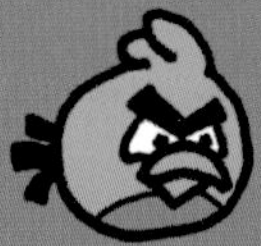

TAKE A DIGITAL DETOX!

POWER DOWN FOR 24 HOURS EVERY WEEK AND SIGN-UP TO THE UNDOLIST.COM

IT'S TIME TO UNPLUG!

ATTACH AN ELASTIC BAND TO YOUR WRIST SO WHEN YOU'RE JONESING TO LOG IN TO FACEBOOK, TWANG THE ELASTIC BAND!

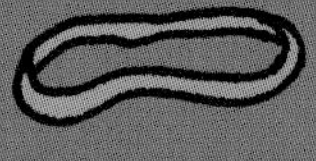

TAKE A DIGITAL DETOX!

TRAIN TO BE A PRIVATE DETECTIVE SO YOU CAN LEGALLY STALK PEOPLE — FOR REAL.

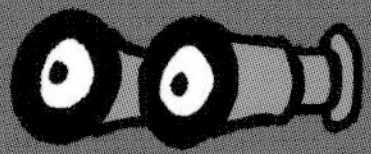

IT'S TIME TO UNPLUG!

JOIN GOOGLE+ INSTEAD.

TAKE A DIGITAL DETOX!

TRY SITTING DOWN WITH YOUR FAMILY TO GIVE THEM AN IN-PERSON STATUS UPDATE ABOUT YOUR DAY!

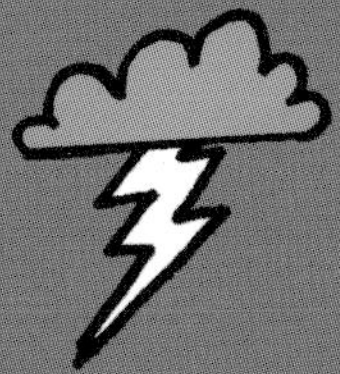

IT'S TIME TO UNPLUG!

GET SENT TO JAIL.

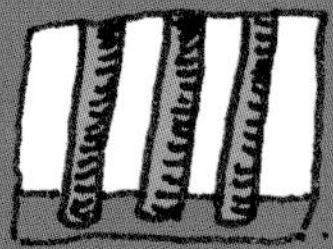

TAKE A DIGITAL DETOX!

COMTEMPLATE THE ZILLIONS YOU'VE HELPED ZUCKERBERG AND CO. MAKE, AND THE CASH YOU'D EARN IF YOU WEREN'T ON FACEBOOK ALL DAY.

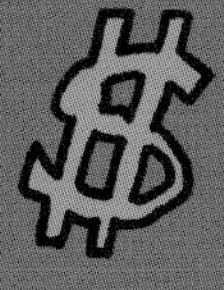

IT'S TIME TO UNPLUG!

IN ORDER TO QUELL ANY NARCISSISTIC WITHDRAWAL SYMPTOMS GET YOUR PROFILE PICTURE PRINTED ON YOUR SHIRT, MUG . . .

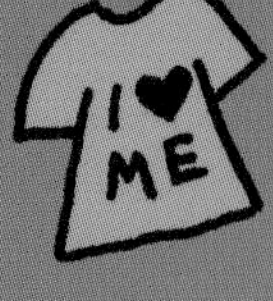
I ♥ ME

TAKE A DIGITAL DETOX!

OR, BECOME AN ACTOR AND GET YOUR FACE WRAPPED ON BILLBOARDS, BUSES, AND MAGAZINE COVERS INSTEAD!

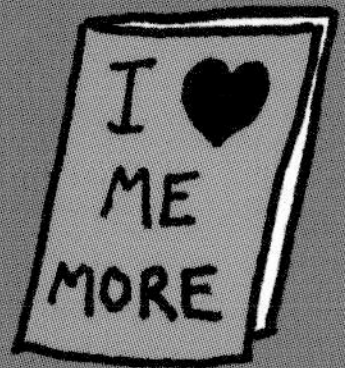
I ♥ ME MORE

IT'S TIME TO UNPLUG!

Donate your laptop to electronicstakeback.com, but first check its real value at buymytronics.com

TAKE A DIGITAL DETOX!

SPEND YOUR FACEBOOK TIME STUDYING ROGET'S THESAURUS FOR SYNONYMS OF "LIKE," IN ORDER TO DEVELOP YOUR VOCABULARY.

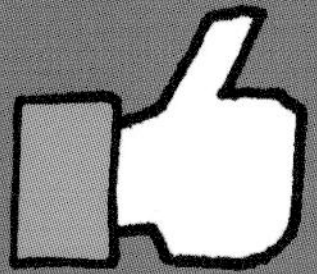

IT'S TIME TO UNPLUG!

Strike a deal with your BF, GF, partner, or parents that for a month of no Facebook use, they give you (delete as applicable):

TAKE A DIGITAL DETOX!

👍 A NEW CAR

✌️ A PAIR OF JIMMY CHOO'S

👌 SEXUAL FAVORS — BUT NOT FROM YOUR PARENTS, PLEASE!

IT'S TIME TO UNPLUG!

Go meditate and connect with your real "self" instead.

TAKE A DIGITAL DETOX!

Forget to pay your electricity bill for ... three months.

IT'S TIME TO UNPLUG!

Download MacFreedom.com to manage the time you spend online.

TAKE A DIGITAL DETOX!

IF ALL ELSE FAILS . . . MOVE TO CHINA!

WITH SPECIAL THANKS TO . . .

A HUGE MEXICAN WAVE OF THANKS GOES OUT TO GUY HOLMES (MY HUBBY), DEANNA LEAH, JOHN WILSON, FINNY FOX-DAVIES, NANCY L. REINHARDT, SCOTT ROSE, JULIA DRAKE, RICHARD WILLIAMS AND GEORGE ADAMS.

MORE ON THE UNPLUG SERIES . . .

VISIT UNPLUGSERIES.COM FOR MORE FUNNY DIGITAL DETOX TIPS AND FUNNY CLIPS OF ADDICTS TAPPING IN TO TECHNOLOGY.

LOOK FOR @FACEBOOKDIET OR TWEET USING #FACEBOOKDIET OR #UNPLUGSERIES

ABOUT THE AUTHOR and ILLUSTRATOR . . .

Gemini Adams has Facebooked for Britain! When not feeding her new Instagram addiction, she can be found writing, drawing, or throwing the ball for her two woofers!

FIND HER AT: GEMINIADAMS.COM

THE END

SHARE YOUR FUNNY SOCIAL MEDIA

ADDICTION STORIES WITH US AT . . .

CONFESSYOURS.COM

GIVE A GIFT

SCAN THE QR CODE WITH YOUR PHONE TO GET A DISCOUNT OR GIFT THIS BOOK TO A FACEBOOK FRIEND!

liveconsciously

LEARN MORE ABOUT OUR BOOKS:

WWW.LIVECONSCIOUSLYNOW.COM

@CONSCIOUSBOOKS